FLAVOURS OF
KOREA

With the Compliments of

The Korea
Foundation

C.P.O.BOX2147 Seoul, KOREA Tel:82-2-753-3462,Fax:82-2-757-2041

D1511022

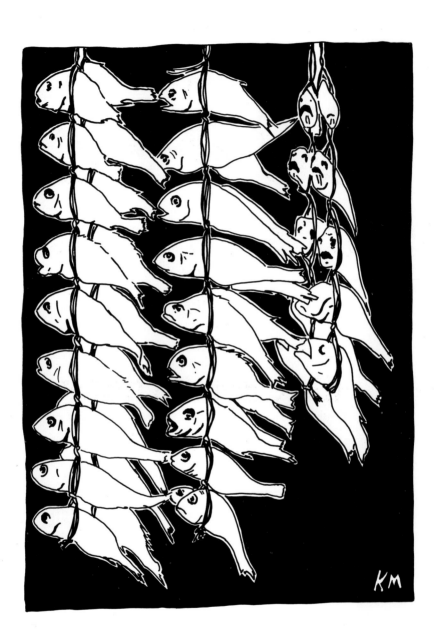

FLAVOURS OF
KOREA

WITH STORIES AND RECIPES
FROM A KOREAN GRANDMOTHER'S
KITCHEN

Marc and Kim Millon

Photographs and drawings
by Kim Millon

ANDRE DEUTSCH

First published in Great Britain in 1991
by André Deutsch Limited
106 Great Russell Street
London WC1B 3LJ

Second impression 1994

British Library Cataloguing in Publication Data
British Library Cataloguing in Publication data
Millon, Kim
Flavours of Korea
I. Food : Korean dishes - Recipes
I. Title II. Millon, Marc
641.595191

ISBN 0 233 98635 9 pbk

Typeset and originated by Setrite Typesetters Limited, Hong Kong
Printed in Hong Kong by Dah Hua Printing Press Co. Limited

To my grandmother

Contents

Preface

My great-grandfather Kim Kyong-bong was a *yangban* – an aristocratic landowner in Yi dynasty Chosun at the turn of the century. The family owned two homes, the main agricultural estate near Pusan, and also a summer house at Sochang, in the cool mountains between Pusan and Ulsan. Already, however, an ancient and proud traditional culture was on the verge of collapse: nonetheless, it was a bold, brave, and defiant act when my grandmother, Bok Dok Sur, then a young girl only sixteen years old, sent her photograph to the American territory of Hawaii, received one in exchange, and by this means, became one of the so-called 'Korean picture brides' and came to a new land to start a new life.

As a young boy growing up on the West Coast of America more than half a century later, those events and places were so far away and distant to me as to be almost non-existent. After all, three generations and a continent are far enough away in time and space. Moreover, third generation Korean on my mother's side, third generation French on my father's, I (and my brother and sister) never really considered ourselves to be anything other than pure American (whatever that is). Korea, its history and culture, remained alien to us, and we, sadly, were ignorant of it.

And yet: did we not have a Korean grandmother whom we called Halmoni (Korean for grandmother) and who spoke mainly Korean to my mother and only broken 'pidgin' English to us? As children, we saw Halmoni often at her home in Los Angeles, and it was there that we always enjoyed the most sumptuous Korean feasts.

Halmoni has always been regarded by her family, friends and business colleagues as a formidable cook. Both before and during the Second World War, she owned and ran a restaurant and saloon in central Honolulu, the Royal Palm Inn, which by all accounts was an extremely popular gathering place for GIs, Koreans, and other islanders alike. Some years later, when Dr Syngman Rhee, the strong-armed nationalist and first president of the newly founded Republic of Korea, came to Los Angeles to thank the Korean Women's Relief Society for its singleminded loyalty during the years of exile while he rallied support against the hated Japanese occupation, it was Halmoni and her friends who cooked for him. 'Ah,' the old reactionary was said to have remarked to her, as he enjoyed her *tubu-tchigae, yachaesanjok*, and *shinsollo*, 'I didn't know that anyone could still prepare the old foods like this.'

Thus, if as children we were perhaps less aware of our cultural background than we should have been, nonetheless, the authentic flavours of Korea were ones that we grew up enjoying with gusto.

One of the only other Korean words that was part of our vocabulary was *kimchi*; even as very young children we loved this hot and crunchy pickled vegetable treat. Indeed, the taste of Halmoni's chilli-tinted cabbage *kimchi* eaten together with large amounts of sticky white rice became as basic — as normal — to me as the taste of french fries and ketchup to my schoolboy friends. *Kimchi*, say some, is a taste that has to be acquired: believe me, it is one worth acquiring.

Pulgogi was another food that we grew up eating probably at least once a week, though we never referred to this Korean national dish of strips of beef marinaded in soy sauce, sesame oil, garlic and ginger, by its proper name. Rather, to us, it was just 'Korean barbecue', though nonetheless delicious for that. Even today, it is still my absolutely favourite food: and I have yet to meet anyone who does not agree that it is fantastic.

Crunchy fresh spinach, dressed in soy sauce and sesame oil; cucumbers soaked in salt water, then squeezed dry and dressed in vinegar, sugar and chilli powder; fried meat fritters; pancakes layered with spring onions, crunchy celery, and strips of beef; meat dumplings in soup; rice, noodles, and much else: these were all authentic Korean foods that we unselfconsciously and ravenously tucked into, without necessarily noticing that they were Korean. For us, they were just home cooking. When we were ill, my mother gave us rice soup (rice boiled into a thick porridge) together with a bit of Korean 'hot meat' to make it go down. On Sundays, we were always treated to 'Korean pancakes', albeit with butter and maple syrup!

Genetic culinary roots must run deep. For why, as Halmoni remembers, when a boy of only five or six, would I pop into her kitchen to sneak pieces of raw, marinading beef. This same raw meat, she says, was one of her father's great favourites. Yet how could I have known then − or even cared − that *yukhoe* is one of the classics of the Korean kitchen?

Halmoni was born in 1907, some three years before the Japanese officially annexed Korea and began their brutal and iron-fisted 'japanization' of the country.

It was not easy for a young girl growing up in those turbulent times. Coming from her traditional and privileged background, she was expected to conform to the neo-Confucian mores and customs relating to the role of females. Women of her class, for example, were not even allowed outside the household compound; they hardly had the opportunity to meet or talk to men; and it was expected that they would submit to arranged marriages when they were fifteen or sixteen years old and then go and live with their husband's families, under the often cruel domination of the mother-in-law.

Halmoni has clear memories of those turbulent times. The March 1st Independence Movement of 1919 was a great historical event, when people all over the country rose up in public demonstrations for independence from the Japanese occupiers. Though only eleven years old at the time, she too was caught up in the groundswell of popular emotion, and marched along with the throngs in Pusan, waving a Korean flag (which had been banned) and shouting '*tongnip mansei!*' − 'long live Korean independence', the cry of freedom. This demonstration, and others throughout the country, were so vast that it is estimated that more than two million Koreans directly took part in them. Halmoni herself was stopped by the police − she was so young, she says, that she hadn't really known what she was doing, but was simply following the emotion and the crowds — but when her stern, conservative father found out, he was furious that his young daughter had strayed from her allotted place in society.

When the old lady matchmakers came to her house, Halmoni was determined not to submit to the fate that had befallen her sisters and friends. So she acted wildly, pulled out her hair, rolled on the floor, and frothed at the mouth. The matchmakers retreated, shaking their heads, and reported negatively to the prospective grooms' families. After such sessions, Halmoni's mother, a tall, beautiful, but stern *yangban*, was furious, and beat her with the brass bowl of her long bamboo pipe.

I wonder why this already very beautiful young woman of only fourteen or fifteen, wanted so much to learn, to travel, to go to far-away lands? How did she have the spirit to rise against centuries of tradition and custom? Even today, Halmoni is an immensely strong character. She was determined to choose and make her own destiny, not fall into some pre-determined and traditional role that she could not accept.

Thus, one day in the early 1920s a woman came to town from Hawaii, searching for 'picture brides' to marry the Korean men who had emigrated to the Hawaiian Islands to work in the pineapple and sugar plantations. Halmoni's mother flew into a rage when she learned of her daughter's intention, and beat her again with the ever-present pipe.

But in reality, in a society where women were hardly valued, and in a family with eight female children to marry, the loss of one in all probability could not have been that great. Three times she tried to leave, but failed. It was a cold bright day in January 1924 when she finally sailed from Pusan first to Kobeo, Japan, then across the Pacific Ocean — the journey took twelve days — to the new world that awaited her.

When Halmoni stepped off the boat in Hawaii, many of the other women who had come to be picture brides wailed, beat their breasts, and in some cases even refused to leave the boat, so disappointed were they when they saw their chosen husbands-to-be. Indeed, Halmoni's had sent her a photograph which showed him to be a young, handsome man when in fact he was now, as she remembers, 'an old man of over forty'. However, Halmoni accepted the situation, for she had not gone there for love — how could she when she had only seen one picture — but rather for the freedom, the adventure which lay before her.

That Halmoni's subsequent marriage to my mother's father

was a great disappointment is all another story. It was always her fate, her *palcha*, she says today ruefully, to be unlucky in love, ever since her mother forbade her to marry her Pusan childhood sweetheart.

She went on to become a leading member of the Korean community in Honolulu, and through hard work — harder, I think, than our generation can ever imagine — and through her remarkable and intuitive business sense, was able to achieve considerable success and female independence in ways that would never have been possible for a woman of her generation in Korea.

Halmoni has been in America for well over sixty years now, but even today Korean remains her native language. Milan Hejtmanek, a close friend and Korean scholar at Harvard's Korea Institute, says that her speech, however, is usually somewhat antiquated and rather formal compared with modern spoken Korean.

Similarly, with Korean cooking, Halmoni still remembers and prepares the old foods in authentically traditional ways, ways which, she says, may even have been forgotten or lost in her native land. At the same time, her taste has inevitably evolved and been influenced not only by the ingredients available to her, but also by Western ways of eating.

Some of the family's favourite dishes were not really Korean at all, it transpires (though they always retained a certain Korean accent): Scotch meat pie (flavoured with a dash of soy sauce), chop steak (a meat, vegetable, and noodle medley based on *chapchae*), and even Irish stew. A truly fine cook, though, is always intuitive. Thus, I am certain that the Korean recipes that Halmoni has shared with us will be readily enjoyed by Westerners, native Koreans and second- or third-generation Koreans alike.

For us, certainly, it has been a joy to work with Halmoni, not least because we enjoy her food so much, but also because it has enabled us to delve into and discover family roots. This book, moreover, has been a real family project. My mother, Lorina Kim, has helped us with many recipes for those second-generation Korean family favourites we grew up eating. Moreover, my mother is an accomplished professional writer and editor, so she helped us extensively in many ways, not least with manuscript preparation, recipe testing, and — no mean task — looking after our rascal son Guy while we struggled to meet our copy deadline.

Uncle Donald Sur has regaled us with stories about Korea for years: indeed, it was he, most of all, who whetted my appetite to learn more about and to visit Korea. As a Fulbright scholar, Donald spent five years in Korea studying both Korean music and Korean mores. A male of good standing in a society obsessed by maleness, he took full advantage of all the country had to offer. Thus he has been a source not only of much useful information, but also inspiration (not that I would ever try to — or hope to — emulate his near-legendary exploits). Uncle Larry Kim, school teacher, writer, photographer, gourmet (he is one of those rare people who has the gift of being able to excel at virtually anything he turns his hand to), has been hugely supportive in all our work. With this project, no less, he has contributed stories as well as recipes — but most of all encouragement and advice.

My sister Michele Millon accompanied the three of us to Korea, a trip we could not have contemplated without her considerable assistance and presence. For us all, it was a real journey: not just halfway across the world, but to a past more dream than reality. Our trip made tangible the bits and pieces garnered over the years from the sometimes elusive, sometimes sharply focused remembrances of our octogenarian grandmother. We were therefore glad to be able to share such wonderful and rare experiences with Michele.

While in Korea, we spent many enjoyable hours and days with my cousin Bong Tae Kim, a well-known Korean-American artist who lives in Los Angeles but teaches part of the year in Seoul. Bong Tae was a most knowledgeable guide, an important source of family stories and background, and simply a fun companion, so we were very fortunate indeed that he was there. Bong Tae more than anyone else is best able to bridge the chasm that yawns between Western and Korean cultures. As the eldest son of my grandmother's only brother, he was able to impart unique family history and details and he fulfilled with respect and love the role of head of our family.

Korean Air assisted us considerably with travel arrangements for which we are most grateful. Mr J. J. Young in London was particularly helpful. While in Korea, the Korea National Tourism Corporation was also helpful in numerous practical ways. Korea, it has to be said, is still very much 'off the beaten track', which makes independent travel both extremely rewarding but also not without its difficulties. Mr Y. I. Kim was both helpful and supportive in advising and assisting us with travel arrangements, and other practical matters. The London office of the KNTC also supported this project from the onset: Anny Hitchings was particularly helpful. There have been many others, too, who

Journal Notes

First Night at the Un Dang Yogwan

Finally arrived after nearly twenty-four hours of travelling: London–Paris–Anchorage–Seoul. Initial impression as we sped into the city centre from Kimpo Airport is that Seoul – with its towering tenement blocks, skyscrapers, and congested traffic – is not all that different from any other modern metropolis. Such thoughts were short-lived, for the brown taxi soon pulled into the courtyard of the Un Dang Yogwan, a famous old traditional inn located in Uni-dong.

Passing through the gateway to the inner courtyard was like walking into another era: the pagoda-roofed buildings were arranged around the courtyard, each with a series of individual, paper-screened cells; on one side there was a larger, more spacious series of rooms (what must formerly have been the anbang *– the main living area), and on another there was a sunken kitchen where we could see women preparing foods over blackened, coal-fired ranges.*

We took off our shoes to enter our tiny room, for the raised floor was spotless and shiny, covered with the most beautiful golden lacquered paper. Apart from some folded bedding and a small table, there was no furniture in the room, so we sat on the warm ondol *floor.*

I asked for some dinner, and before long the boy returned, carrying a small, low table laden with no less than sixteen round dishes, bowls and saucers: there were two types of kimchi, *one, a quite fantastic hot and sour winter* kimchi, *and the other, an altogether milder* nabakkimchi: *fresh, crunchy slices of radish and cabbage in water. There was also a selection of* namul: muusaengchae, chui *and* sigumchinamul; *some strips of meat in* kochujang; *a piece of dried pollock fried in batter; a pile of crisp* tasima *– strips of kelp deep-fried in sesame oil; bowls of* twoenjangtchigae, *a soupy bean paste and curd stew.*

We washed this remarkable repast down with poricha. *Then, exhausted, we spread out our bedding on the warm* ondol *floor: a* yo *– that is, a* futon-*like mattress – and colourful* ibul *quilts. Our pillows were hard and cylindrical, filled with rice husks, but they were quite up to the job. Guy lay on a sheepskin spread out between us and we all slept wonderfully well.*

helped us considerably with this project – too many to mention individually: we take this opportunity to thank them all.

We would also like to thank Elise Simon Goodman; our agent Dieter Klein; and our editor Laura Morris for her enthusiasm, understanding and kindness.

It has always been our belief that food is one basic and approachable avenue which allows us to enter into and discover cultures different from our own. *Flavours of Korea* has been very much a voyage of discovery for both of us. The foods of Korea, for Kim, could hardly provide a greater contrast to those of England, yet she has come to love them nevertheless (did she really ever have any choice?). For me, it has been a wonderful and satisfying experience to voyage both into my grandmother's and our family's past, as well as to work out and share recipes for foods that I love with a broader audience.

Korea, until recently, has been a curiously overlooked country — indeed perhaps even a misunderstood country. It is our fervent hope that this book will introduce many newcomers not only to the satisfying delights of the flavours of Korea, but also to the richness of its culture, history, and people.

Topsham, Devon, England

Hangul: The Korean Phonetic Alphabet

Hangul, the Korean alphabet, is a unique and remarkable system of writing developed during the reign of King Sejong, fourth ruler of the Yi dynasty, and introduced to the royal court in 1443. Prior to this, there was no adequate way of depicting Korean thought and language in written form. The only method available was a somewhat tortured rendition of Korean through the use of Chinese characters. But Korean and Chinese are totally dissimilar and unrelated languages.

Sejong therefore devised an alphabetic system utilizing twenty-eight letters based on phonetics and human physiology — that is, on the actual shape of the mouth when speaking. It is an ingenious system, and remarkably simple: Sejong boasted that a clever person could learn *hangul* in a morning and even foolish people could understand it after only ten days of study.

There are at least two widely used forms for transliterating written Korean, and even in Korea itself, there may be little consistency: some road signs, for example, point you to Busan, others to Pusan, the nation's second city. The most widely accepted form of transliteration is the McCune—Reischauer. We have broadly tried to stay as close as possible to this. However, since diacritical marks and other unnecessary punctuation have little relevance to the general reader, we have omitted them. Koreans, scholars, linguists and philologists, we hope, will not be overly critical of this omission or of any inconsistencies of spelling for which we are wholly responsible.

Mini-Glossary to Some Basic Korean Dishes and Terms

Kimchi Virtually the national dish of pickled vegetables, usually first salted, then seasoned. There are countless varieties, though the most common consists of salted Korean cabbage layered with garlic, ginger, chilli pepper, and salted or fermented fish, prawns or oysters.

Namul The generic term for seasoned vegetables, sometimes served raw, stir-fried, lightly steamed, or boiled. **Namuls** are served at every Korean meal, and are made with any number of vegetables, as well as with wild roots, sprouts, stems and leaves.

Gui Barbecued or grilled food, often cooked at the table over a burner or charcoal. **Pulgogi**, Korean-style marinated barbecued beef, is the most famous such dish.

Guk or Tang Soup or stew.

Pab Rice, the everyday staple of Korea.

Chongol Korean one-pot stew, usually a combination of meat, fish, beancurd and/or vegetables, often cooked at the table over a burner. Similar to Japanese *sukiyaki*.

Jon Batter-fried vegetables, meat or fish. **Pajon** — green onion pancake — is the best known of many varieties.

Pokkum Stir-fried or braised dish. **Nakchibokkum**, stir-fried baby octopus is a popular snack.

Shinsollo Splendid medley of meat, fish, vegetables and gingko nuts prepared in a special *shinsollo* pot kept warm with charcoal in its chimney. A dish formerly eaten only by royalty.

Kujolpan Nine-sectioned lacquerware dish filled with mixtures of meat, seasoned vegetables, fish and pancakes: another example of elegant, refined, palace food.

1
Korea, the Country and Food

If the food of a country is determined by its geography then Korean cuisine aptly reflects the terrain of a harsh peninsula bounded by water everywhere except the north, and rippled with surprisingly large mountains extending down virtually the whole of its thousand-kilometre-long spine, from southern Manchuria even to offshore Cheju island.

To the west lies the Yellow Sea, stretching out between Korea and the shores of mainland China. Throughout this vast, shallow body of water, here and all along the south coast, there are literally thousands of islands, many of which are inhabited, as well as countless inlets and craggy harbours where scores of fishing boats ply their trade. The famous Hallyo waterway runs from south of Pusan along the coast, following a ribbon of stepping-stone islands, submerged mountains, only their peaks showing now, in endless succession linking Chungmu, Yosu, Masan, and Chinhae. These warmer, shallow waters are a particularly rich and fertile source of shellfish and seaweed.

In contrast, the East Sea is altogether deeper, more profound, its colder water yielding great catches of deepwater fish, squid and cuttlefish. Driving along this eastern seaboard, one is reminded strangely of the Californian coast between Los Angeles and San Francisco — except that here, along virtually the entire route, the beaches are fenced off by chain link and barbed wire, a reminder of the very real and still constant fear of invasion from the north.

These great stretches of coastline provide Koreans with a plentiful and astounding array of fish, shellfish, and other edible sea creatures. Red snapper, herring, cod, croaker, spanish mackerel, tuna, sea bass, corvina, halibut, skate, sole, and pollock are all plentiful and popular, as are oysters, squid, cuttlefish, octopus, prawns, a wide variety of clams, sea cucumbers, sea squirt, sea snails, whelks, abalone, mussels, and scores of other unusual sea creatures. And as Western countries are coming to discover sea vegetation as a bountiful food source of the future (with ocean agronomy a major field of study and research) the Koreans have for centuries harvested and consumed with delight many varieties of seaweed.

Inland, on the flatter lowlands and plains of the south, great tracts of land are given over to agriculture and the cultivation of vegetables, fruits, nuts, and grains (rice certainly as well as millet, sorghum, and barley). The steeper mountains, on the other hand, that cover most of the country, are an important source of wild vegetables, herbs, roots, and funghi. Korea is located in the temperate zone, and thus has four distinct seasons. Most of the annual rainfall comes in spring and summer, ideal for the cultivation of rice. Winter can be surprisingly bitter.

For centuries, the staple diet of the ordinary Korean has consisted of rice, dried or pickled fish, pickled vegetables, and precious little else. Drying fish, of course, is a traditional method of preserving it over winter. The harsh climate of the Korean peninsula has meant that such foods had to be put aside for those times when fresh ingredients were not available. But even today, when modern transport means that fresh fish is within reach of all, just as in Mediterranean countries where the consumption of salt cod remains a staple, so in Korea one finds dried fish, cuttlefish, and shrimp, as well as an amazing array of pickled seafood — oysters in *kochujang*, soused shrimp, pickled octopus, salted pollock roe, pickled cod's roe and much else — eaten out of choice, not necessity.

This same need for preserved foods that could last out the hard winter led to the development of *kimchi*, unique in the world's catalogue of national dishes. *Kimchi* is no more than pickled and preserved vegetables, fish, meat, or combinations thereof, which, once fermented in immense earthenware jars, could be left outside buried in the ground or insulated in straw huts for months at a time. Yet what variation exists within this simple equation! Like dried fish, *kimchi* became the staple of the Korean diet many centuries if not millennia ago, and still remains so today. For in Korea, tastes die hard, and it would surely be a brave wife who attempted to serve her husband a meal without *kimchi*! Indeed, it used to be said that a woman's worth was

> ## *Ondol*: A Unique and Exceptional Form of Heating
> The harsh Korean climate led to the early development of the *ondol* form of central heating, one of the world's oldest, and still one of the most effective. Basically, in a traditional Korean house, the kitchen with its wood- or coal-fired range remains at floor level or is sunk somewhat into the earth, while the living rooms, the *anbang* and *sarangbang*, are raised above this level. Underneath the floors of these living areas, a system of flues extends from the kitchen range to a final outdoor chimney. Thus, the exhaust from the range passes through the flues, heating in turn large paving slabs, themselves covered with lacquered paper. This paper floor, smooth, shiny, and yellowed with age, glows with warmth, heat and comfort, and it is here that the Koreans live, simply, and close to the earth.

measured by the quality of her *kimchi*, and to a certain extent, this is still probably true. (Feminism has not yet made much headway in Korea.)

Kimchi and pickled or soused fish are strong foods which have traditionally been counterbalanced by large quantities of steamed white rice, undoubtedly still the staple food of the nation. Koreans are great rice eaters, and, bland though this starch may seem to Westerners, it is a food often enjoyed in its own right. The cultivation of rice has always been an important feature of Korean agriculture: indeed, the pattern of the days and years could be measured in part by the planting and harvesting of rice.

It may seem surprising, given the mountainous make-up of the land, that beef traditionally has been and remains the favourite meat of Koreans. Indeed, Halmoni says that as a child, she had never even laid eyes on a pig. Pigs were more prevalent in the north, apparently, but cattle were raised all over the rest of the country, the good red beef they provided to be marinaded with soy sauce, garlic, sesame oil, and ginger for meaty feasts of *pulgogi*, *kalbi*, and as a base for stews and soups. Could this penchant for beef be a genetic inheritance from the palates of those nomadic, meat-loving tribes who settled in the peninsula so many thousands of years ago?

> ## The *Jang* Terrace
> The *jang* terrace, a stone area outside a country house, or, in cities, a section of an apartment balcony, or even an area of roof, is still an important feature of most households. In this area stand large earthenware jars, kept as receptacles for the three most important staple elements of the Korean kitchen: *kanjang* (soy sauce), *twoenjang* (fermented soy bean paste), and *kochujang* (red pepper, soy bean and glutinous rice paste). Every household used to ferment their own soy beans and make their own sauces, enough to fill the jars and last months or even a whole year. Indeed, in the past, it was possible to measure someone's wealth by the number of storage jars displayed on their *jang* terrace. Even today, the pervasive and hardly delicate smell of homemade *twoenjang* is the characteristic aroma of Seoul and elsewhere.

The Korean peninsula is, of course, divided today, but the yearning for reunification is an indication of how strongly the Korean national identity remains intact, in spite of the tragic events of this century alone. Kim Il Sung's Democratic People's Republic of Korea, better known to us as North Korea, is a closed and introverted society, little visited by people from the outside world. Nonetheless, it is quite probable that the food eaten there is on the whole much the same as that in the south, though with some regional variations of course. Kaesong *kimchi* (Kaesong, once the capital of the Koryo dynasty, now a small provincial town located in North Korea) is much enjoyed south of the demilitarized zone, perhaps partly out of nostalgia as much as for the fact that it really is so delicious.

Generally speaking, the further south one travels on the peninsula, the saltier, hotter, and spicier the foods become, a phenomenon true elsewhere in the world, on the Indian sub-continent, in some Mediterranean countries, and in Meso-America, for example, probably because hot foods encourage perspiration, the body's natural method of cooling itself. The Cholla provinces, located in the southwest corner of the country, are generally regarded as foremost centres of gastronomy. The food of Kwangju is undoubtedly hot and fiery, a reflection perhaps of the hot-blooded spirit of this rebellious regional capital. And in nearby Chonju, famous above all for its exquisite rice medley *pibimbap*, it is not just the quality of the dishes but indeed the quantity — the sheer array of *panchan* — side dishes — that is most astounding.

Geography and climate do indeed have considerable bearing on a national cuisine. Social factors also determine how and what a people eat. In Korea, as in other nations with a highly developed system of social stratification, there has always been a contrast between the hearty and robust foods of the people, and the more refined culinary traditions which came down from the tables of the aristocracy and the royal court. The tradition of Yi dynasty palace foods is a particularly rich and distinctive one. *Shinsollo*, a fabulous and many-layered hot-pot, for example, was so special a century ago that it could only be prepared for and eaten by the royal family.

Korean Food

One of the finest features of the Korean table is that it is invariably laid with a sumptuous array of *panchan* — side dishes, bowls, saucers, and plates all bearing different and delicious morsels. Indeed, a simple family meal might have as many as twenty bowls and dishes on the table. Only poor people, says Halmoni, would eat one dish with rice. When her Korean friends first came over to visit her in Hawaii, they were astounded, not to say dismayed, at Western ways. 'Americans so rich,' they said to her after eating a meal that consisted of only one plate of meat, rice, and vegetables, 'but why do they eat so poor?'

There are indeed certain essentials without which no Korean meal would be complete. Every person always has his/her own rice bowl, usually lidded and made of metal, filled with steamed white rice or rice mixed with other grains or vegetables.

Kimchi in at least one form — and preferably in two, three or even more varieties — is always on the table. Soups, *guk* or *tang*, are also important features, eaten at every meal, while *namuls* — bowls of seasoned raw or slightly steamed vegetables — should also always be included, together, perhaps, with fried foods — *jon* — and with other side dishes such as salted fish cut into thin strips and seasoned, toasted seaweed, and any number of other dishes made with dried vegetables, meat, or fish. Even substantial dishes of meat, stews, fish, or poultry are often served in small bowls, for they are primarily foods to be eaten in conjunction with all of the other *panchan*, rather than as a main course of a meal.

Indeed, 'main foods' as we tend to think of them, don't usually hold such central pride of place in the scheme of everyday Korean meals. Eating Korean-style consists more of 'grazing' over the whole range of foods displayed on the table, picking a bit of this, nibbling a bit of that, sampling some bean curd soup and a spoonful of rice, crunching on a bit of *kimchi*, then choosing again whatever strikes one's fancy. Certainly, foods such as *pulgogi*, *kalbi*, or *chongol* (a Korean version of *sukiyaki*), placed on burners in the middle of the table, take pride of place. But even so, the quality of a meal may still be measured not by what we would consider a so-called main course but rather by the range and quality of side dishes which accompany it.

This diversity and range highlights another essential tenet of Korean dining — the importance of balance. No single food or flavour should dominate. Fiery *kimchi* is balanced by steamed white rice; batter-fried *jon* is deliciously complemented by crunchy, soy-and-sesame dressed greens; seafresh raw fish and shellfish are perfect counterpoints to tasty, savoury barbecued meats. Whatever the components of a Korean meal, this essential balance of foods and flavours must always be maintained.

░░░░░░░░░░ Korean Food '*Haole*' style ░░░░░░░░░░

Halmoni often uses the world *haole* in her vocabulary. It is not a Korean word, but rather pure Hawaiian, and it means 'foreigner', that is, non-Hawaiian. When she uses it, though, it really means non-Korean, or Western. Though we are her grandchildren, Halmoni has always considered us to be *haoles* (since our father is): but the word as she uses it is only mildly pejorative.

Halmoni is the first to admit that preparing and eating foods in authentic Korean style day in and day out is a labour-intensive task. Unless you are prepared to make varieties of *kimchi* regularly, and to have a store of *panchan* — *namul saengchae*, *muchim*, and so on — on hand for each meal, then it is difficult, if not impossible, to present the ample array of foods with which an authentic

Korean Etiquette: Don't Blow Your Nose!

Korea, with its strong neo-Confucian tradition, is still by any standards a formal country, and the visitor should be aware of certain protocols. Naturally, one takes off one's shoes upon entering a Korean house, or an *ondol* dining room. The most honoured guest — or the eldest person — is usually seated midway along the table, furthest from the door and away from any draft (the host, in contrast, might himself sit in that humble position).

One always offers and receives — whether gifts or a glass of wine — with both hands (or with one hand stylistically placed on the forearm), and one never pours one's own drink. While eating, chopsticks should never be left *in* the rice bowl; if only pausing during the meal, then they should be laid on top of the bowl; and when one is finished, the chopsticks should be laid on the table.

Making slurping noises while eating is considered a sign of appreciation. Likewise, after eating, a good healthy belch is also a means of indicating that you have eaten well. (Genetic roots must run deep, for our cousin Matthew has been following this custom since he was an infant, to the sometimes considerable consternation of his Aunt, my mother, whenever he comes to our house to eat.) Admittedly, when in a crowded restaurant in Korea, this custom can be somewhat unnerving to the uninitiated. But don't be shy: by all means, if you feel so inclined, join in the general happy cacophony and let slurp or burp; you may never know such freedom again.

Korean food, undoubtedly, is spicy to say the least, and those not accustomed to it may find that it will make one's eyes water or nose run. However, one thing you must never do is to blow your nose at the dinner table. If necessary excuse yourself to another room, or else suffer in silence. To do otherwise is to immediately place yourself — in Korean eyes — in the category of a *sangnom* — an unperson, hardly worthy of consideration.

Korean table is laid, for such foods simply cannot be made from scratch whenever you decide to eat 'Korean style'. Moreover, here we eat off plates rather than bowls, and we are undoubtedly more accustomed to eating larger quantities of main course food than is the case in Korea.

Halmoni, then, has over the years undoubtedly adapted her way of eating — if not the flavourings of the food she prepares. For example, she says that she likes to use a lot of meat when she prepares dishes like *chongol* or *chapchae*, much more, say, than would be the case for the same foods prepared in Korea. Meat,

Korean Pancakes

True Korean breakfasts differ little from Korean dinners, and consist of the same spread of rice, soup, *kimchi*, and *panchan* eaten at other meals. Yet as children we always enjoyed a breakfast of 'Korean pancakes'. What is it, I always wondered, that makes these delicious, large, chewy pancakes Korean? I conjecture now that Halmoni probably devised her version from the basic Korean fritter or *jon* batter, but wanting to integrate herself into her new culture, served it Western style, an example of how foods from different cultures fuse to become something new and unique. Whatever the exact provenance, we always enjoyed 'Korean pancakes' for breakfast every Sunday, while listening to *Don Giovanni* or *The Magic Flute*. Thus fortified, we tackled the fat Sunday newspapers.

Korean Pancakes

1 large egg
6 tablespoons milk
$\frac{1}{3}$ pint (200 ml) water
1 tablespoon sugar (optional)
$\frac{1}{2}$ lb (250 g) flour
1 tablespoon vegetable oil
Pinch of salt
Cooking oil for frying

Mix the ingredients together lightly, taking care not to overbeat. Leave to rest for half an hour. The batter should be fairly runny. Heat a heavy-bottomed frying pan until very hot. Rub the pan with an oil-soaked paper towel to grease, then ladle just enough batter to spread thinly over the entire surface. Cook and turn over pancake when dark bubbles appear. Serve with butter and maple syrup.

after all, is still plentiful and comparatively inexpensive, and she has never stinted on it.

Conversely, when Halmoni cooks Western food, we usually find that they are often and unselfconsciously served with an unmistakable Korean accent: beautiful rare prime rib, served with potatoes, steamed broccoli and *kimchi*; hamburgers spiked with chillies and sesame seeds; or fresh vegetables — whatever is available — steamed and dressed in *chojang* — vinegar soy sauce.

It is never possible to transpose fully and recreate a national cuisine outside that nation, and over the years and generations, foods and tastes do change and adapt. From our point of view, it is quite possible — and delicious — to enjoy eating Korean foods '*haole* style' as Halmoni would say, or Western style. Indeed this is how we unselfconsciously grew up enjoying them. For example, *pulgogi* is just Korean barbecue to us, as common a food as, but far superior to, barbecued burgers or hot dogs. We have always liked it best served not with a wide array of Korean *panchan*, but rather with steamed buttered rice mixed with peas or chopped parsley, and a fresh green salad, dressed with vinegar and oil.

Many of the foods in this book can be enjoyed '*haole* style', eaten as a main course rather than as one in an array of other dishes. Likewise, Korean-style vegetables, lightly steamed and dressed in soy sauce and sesame oil, or crunchy, fresh Korean salads are perfectly in tune with today's tastes and eating habits, and ought certainly to be incorporated into everyone's repertoire.

But that said, do take time, now and then, to prepare and present a full Korean meal, in all its delicious and splendid variety.

A Note on Quantities and Measurements

Because Korean foods are usually meant to be eaten in conjunction with a large array of other side dishes, it is almost impossible to say adequately how many people they will serve. It all depends, not only on who is eating but on what else is being served. However, as a general rule, and unless otherwise mentioned, most of the recipes in this book are written for two to four adequate portions if eaten as part of a meal '*haole* style' — if served as part of an authentic Korean spread, then they could serve as many as four to eight, depending on the number of other courses served. All measurements are given first in imperial then metric equivalents. When 'cup' is used as in Chapter 6, it can be taken to mean 4 oz (125 g). It is important to use either metric or imperial measurements throughout a recipe.

2
Techniques, Equipment and Ingredients

Techniques

The preparation of Korean foods is not difficult once basic techniques are mastered, but since so many dishes are generally served at a Korean meal there is inevitably considerable time and effort involved. Of course, this is a carry-over from those days when a woman's main daily task was the preparation and serving of food. And since traditional Korean breakfasts are little different from Korean dinners (lunch is usually a somewhat lighter meal, perhaps just a bowl of *pibimbap* or noodles), this meant the women of the house had to rise early to begin cooking.

Even nowadays, as when we stayed in the Un Dang Yogwan, a traditional inn in central Seoul, we were awakened as early as 5.00 a.m. by noises from the central sunken kitchen across the courtyard from our room. Our sumptuous breakfast that day consisted of no fewer than sixteen plates and bowls, including three different types of *kimchi* — a little hard to handle at eight in the morning!

Of course, not everyone breakfasts daily in this fashion: indeed, in Seoul, many people nowadays prefer simple Western breakfasts of cereal or toast and coffee. Since so many women themselves go out to work, it is not surprising that these changes have taken place; indeed, it is a pattern being adopted throughout the developed and developing world as traditional roles are confronted by accelerating social change.

Even so, preparing just an evening meal, Korean-style, is a considerable task, let alone the larger family banquets often enjoyed at weekends. And even Korean picnics can be most elaborate affairs, with burners transported to outdoor areas for the cooking of rice, soups, or stews.

Knives

Halmoni wanted to give me her favourite knife but, she told me, it is bad luck to give someone a knife as a present. Once she gave a daughter-in-law a knife and (says Halmoni) she turned against her. On another occasion a friend gave Halmoni a knife and Halmoni has never since felt the same about her. So when she came to give me the knife, she said, 'First pay me one dollar.' I handed it over and she gave me the knife. 'There. I sold you my knife,' she said. 'There will be no bad blood between us.'

Since the only implements used by the Koreans are a pair of chopsticks (usually metal or wood, round and pointed almost like knitting needles) and a spoon (long-handled and with a round, rather flat bowl), it is important that all ingredients are chopped into small, manageable pieces.

Indeed chopping and slicing is one of the main time-consuming tasks in preparing Korean food. Vegetables like carrots, courgettes, or thin, narrow aubergines, are sliced not straight but diagonally. Spring onions, used extensively in the Korean kitchen, may be sliced, shredded, or, more frequently, cut into diagonal slivers. When preparing a number of foods to be cooked together, it is important that the ingredients are sliced about the same size so that they will cook evenly. Meats, if not sliced into small pieces, are usually scored to allow seasonings and marinades to penetrate. For rather tough pieces of meat, such as *kalbi* (short ribs) as well as for chicken pieces, the scoring should be deep, all the way to the bone, to allow maximum absorption.

'Hands on' Cooking

The preparation of Korean food is a 'hands on' job. Put on an apron, roll up your sleeves and get stuck in. Don't try delicately to stir a bowl of marinading beef: plunge your hands in and firmly massage in the seasonings. Beat eggs, not with a fork or a wire whisk, but with your bare hands (less air gets in and they then stick better to what they are coating). Wash pots of uncooked rice vigorously to get out all the excess starch; wring out colanders of steamed spinach or watercress, tightly squeezing out all the excess moisture with your hands. Pick up and inspect your ingredients; feel them, look at them to make sure they are fresh and of the highest quality. Korean cuisine is nothing if not robust and direct: its preparation calls for similarly bold and forthright techniques.

꜀꜀꜀꜀꜀꜀꜀꜀꜀꜀꜀꜀꜀ **Equipment** ꜀꜀꜀꜀꜀꜀꜀꜀꜀꜀꜀꜀꜀

The kitchen of a traditional *ondol* house is generally found at or below ground level. The *yontan*-fired ranges (*yontan* are anthracite coal bricks, the commonest form of fuel available in Korea) generally have two or four cooking burners, and the flues pass underneath the living areas creating the *ondol* system of central heating. The variety of foods that can be prepared in such primitive kitchens is outstanding, but, as mentioned already, is achieved not without a considerable amount of time and hard manual labour.

Though little specialized equipment is necessary to prepare Korean foods, city dwellers in Seoul, Pusan, Honolulu, London or Los Angeles, on the other hand, do take advantage of modern and labour-saving devices.

Electric Rice Cooker: In a country where rice may be cooked fresh at least twice or even three times a day, electric rice cookers are essential and common pieces of equipment (as common, say, as the ever-present electric kettle in Britain). They come in sizes ranging from small (two to four cups) to immense professional-sized cookers used by restaurants. Not only do electric rice cookers cook rice perfectly every time, but they are also able to keep it warm for considerable periods without it drying out or overcooking.

Electric Frying Pan: Fried *jon* — dishes made from ingredients or mixtures of ingredients dipped first in flour then in egg — are particularly popular and delicious. Though exceedingly simple, the art of frying well so that the ingredients stay crisp and fresh on the inside and cook crisply on the outside calls for a certain amount of intuitive skill. An electric frying pan certainly eases the task, and is well worth investing in. The oil can be kept at an even temperature so that foods neither burn nor cook suddenly in oil that is not hot enough. And they are generally large enough to take a number of fritters at once.

Table-top Burners, Brass Shields, Meat Grids: There is nothing Koreans like better than cooking foods directly at the table. *Pulgogi, kalbi* and *chongol* all taste better when cooked in front of you, the anticipation as much part of the enjoyment as the eating. Small portable table-top burners which utilize disposable gas canisters are popular in homes and restaurants alike (always ensure that there is adequate ventilation), and they can be purchased from Korean and Chinese groceries. Brass *pulgogi* shields, and metal grids for cooking meat and fish directly over the flames, are also useful. Alternatively, use an outdoor barbecue.

Grater or Food Processor: For the preparation of grated or sliced vegetables for salads and *namul*, a good basic grater or food processor is essential. Halmoni uses a manual grater which fits over a plastic receptacle, and this works well for long, thin narrow strips of *muu* (Korean radish), or for thin almost transparent slices of cucumber. Once when we were preparing a large family supper, sister-in-law Joan was given the task of grating a pile of enormous Korean radishes. After she laboured over the manual grater for some minutes, she suggested that she bring over her food processor. Halmoni was most sceptical, shook her head, and said that it would not be the same, but Joan was her equal in persistence. She set up the food processor, and within seconds had grated all the radishes. Halmoni suspiciously examined the result, but reluctantly had to agree that it passed muster.

Kitchen Scissors: Because Korean food is eaten with chopsticks, it is essential that the foods are prepared in small or bite-sized pieces. This may not always be the case, and in such instances, kitchen scissors are useful to have on hand. When *kalbi* is prepared at the table, for example, it can be snipped into smaller pieces. Or, when *naengmyon* (cold buckwheat noodles) or other noodles are eaten, they too might be snipped into more manageable lengths.

Oriental Pestle and Mortar and/or Heavy Metal Meat Hammer: Oriental pestles and mortars are serrated on the inside, and are useful for crushing toasted sesame seeds or for pounding garlic and ginger. Alternatively, pound the garlic and ginger with a heavy metal meat hammer. Incidentally, since so much garlic and ginger is used in Korean cooking it is well worth preparing it all before you begin cooking. Crush and chop sufficient for all your recipes, and store separately in small dishes or screw-top jars until ready to use. A metal meat hammer is also useful for pounding meat to tenderize it, especially necessary for meats to be cooked on the barbecue.

Shinsollo: *Shinsollo*, a very special dish once eaten only by royalty, is prepared in its own pot, which has a chimney in the middle where pieces of charcoal are placed to keep the whole mixture sizzling. Such pots are certainly worth investing in if you are going to prepare this speciality from time to time; similar versions of hot pots may also be available from Chinese food specialists.

Table Utensils: The principal table utensils for a Korean meal are an individual rice bowl, a Korean spoon, and a pair of pointed metal or wooden chopsticks for each diner. Foods are usually presented on the table in a collection of small bowls and dishes. Depending on how many are at the table, dishes of *kimchi* and *namul* are shared by every three or four diners. *Poricha*, rice tea, or tea is drunk out of china cups, though if available celadon vessels are of course the most elegant. *Kujolpan*, a special appetizer, is served in a beautiful nine-compartment lacquerware container.

꙰꙰꙰꙰꙰꙰꙰꙰꙰꙰꙰ **Ingredients** ꙰꙰꙰꙰꙰꙰꙰꙰꙰꙰꙰

Below is a selective alphabetical glossary of ingredients used in the Korean kitchen. Highlighted in **bold print** are all those items essential to your store cupboard.

Acorn curd (*totori muk*): Gelatinous curd made from acorns. Sold in cakes or slabs, ready to eat. Rather bland but much loved by Koreans.

Aubergine (*kaji*): A popular vegetable — Korean varieties are generally long and very thin.

Bamboo shoots: Tender bamboo shoots are sometimes available fresh (if so, they need to be blanched in boiling water before use), but are more often encountered in tins. Choose those containing large or whole pieces, not already sliced shoots.

Bean curd (*tubu*): Soy bean curd is one of the most important daily elements in the Korean diet, used as an ingredient in soups and stews, deep-fried or pan-fried, or braised in meat sauce. It is high in protein and extremely nutritious. Keep soy bean cakes in a refrigerator in a bowl of water that is changed daily. Fresh soy bean curd (*sundubu*) can be made at home.

Bean sprouts (*kongnamul*): Large bean sprouts from yellow soy beans and smaller sprouts from mung beans are eaten regularly at most meals. Ensure that sprouts are really fresh, not yellow or wilted. Alternatively, sprout them yourself at home.

Beans (*kong*): Beans form an important part of the Korean diet: yellow soy beans, black soy beans, mung beans, aduki beans, and red and black kidney beans are all popular. Ground mung bean flour can be used to make *chongpo muk* (mung bean curd), while coarsely ground mung beans are used to make *pindaettok*, a delicious, crunchy fritter.

Chestnuts: Both fresh and dried chestnuts are eaten extensively in Korea: roasted, and used as an ingredient to add to stews, or made into delicious glazed or mashed sweets.

Dried and wild vegetables and roots: In mountain and wooded areas, and in favourable seasons, Koreans everywhere are on the look-out for wild vegetables and roots to make into delicious *namul*. However, at other times of the year, dried vegetables and roots are available, and are enjoyed by all. In addition to the best known and popular varieties below, Korean grocers may also stock a range of other dried vegetables, including dried sweet potato stems, dried green pepper leaves, dried sliced radish, dried lotus root, dried garlic stems, dried sea mustard stems, and much else. Dried ingredients are handy to have in a store cupboard, for they can then be reconstituted to be made into tasty *namul* — dressed in soy sauce and sesame oil — most easily.

Kosari: Tender brown bracken shoots and fern stems are extremely popular. The larger, softer, so-called royal fern variety is in fact the popular fiddlehead green. Fresh fiddleheads, if available, can be quickly blanched then dressed to make a superb and unusual *namul*.

Toraji: This white rootlet from the edible mountain bellflower is particularly delicious fresh, dressed in chilli, vinegar, and

---

Korean 'Health Foods'
It is an indictment of our Western diet that so called 'health food' shops are now an important and permanent feature of the food scene, for the implication clearly is that our normal diet is not healthy.

In the Korean scheme of things, though, there is little difference between food eaten for sustenance and food eaten for health. Indeed the daily diet should serve not only to nourish us but to promote and maintain beneficial balances, an equilibrium between *um* (or *yin*) and *yang*, resulting in a healthy body and mind.

I believe that the Korean diet, with its emphasis on lightly blanched vegetables; whole grains, nuts, seeds, and beans; bean curd; and small amounts of meat, fish, and shellfish, is inherently in tune with those nutritional concerns that we in the West have today. (My only reservations lie in the amount of salt and white sugar consumed.) Therefore, those who may not have a Korean or oriental grocery nearby, should consider the range of 'Korean' foods that are available in most health food shops: grains such as millet, barley, buckwheat, and sorghum; soy beans, mung beans, aduki beans, and other beans; bean curd; bean paste; pine nuts; sesame seeds; soy sauce; buckwheat noodles; and a range of seaweeds, to mention a few.

sesame oil. Dried *toraji* is also widely available, and is a popular and special favourite.

Todok: A large hairy root that must be pounded then sliced before being seasoned with *kochujang* and — usually — grilled over charcoal.

Turup: Young, tender shoots of the angelica bush are great delicacies, gathered in springtime only and par-boiled to be eaten like asparagus, or else fried in batter.

Uong: *Uong*, or burdock, is another stalky, popular root that must be peeled, scalded, then cooked with meat and soy sauce. Dried burdock is widely available and a popular ingredient for *namul*.

Chui: An edible wild mountain green that is treated, like spinach or watercress, by par-boiling or steaming (if fresh). Dried *chui* must be soaked first then dressed in soy sauce and sesame oil.

Fruit: Korean meals normally end with a plate of fresh fruit, not surprising considering how good Korean fruit is. The most distinctive native fruit is the Korean pear (*pae*), a large, brown-skinned orb that is incredibly juicy and crisp. The Korean (or Asian) pear is sometimes available in this country. Apples (*sagwa*) from Taegu are also famous, while strawberries (*ttalgi*) and other soft fruit are also greatly enjoyed. Persimmons (*kam*) are another sticky favourite (Halmoni remembers the orchard of persimmon trees at their summer house); dried persimmons (*kotgam*) which may be available from Korean grocers, make a wonderful and refreshing fruit punch, *sujonggwa*.

Garland chrysanthemum (*ssukka*): A characteristic and unusual vegetable, enjoyed both raw and steamed and dressed as *namul*. The garland chrysanthemum is no relation to the more familiar flower, which can be poisonous, so do not subsititute!

Garlic (*manul*): One of the most important and characteristic flavourings of the Korean kitchen, widely used in marinades, in dressings, and even grilled in whole cloves alongside *pulgogi* or *kalbi*. Garlic is usually pounded before being chopped to further release its oils and aroma.

Ginger root (*saenggang*): Fresh ginger root is another essential flavouring widely used in most Korean dishes. Choose roots that are not too knobbly since they must be peeled before being pounded and chopped. To keep ginger, wrap in a moist piece of kitchen paper, then in cellophane, and store in the refrigerator. Powdered ginger is never an adequate substitute for fresh ginger.

Gingko nuts (*unhaeng*): The gingko tree is a symbol of Korea, and indeed the nuts which it yields are equally special, used as a garnish for festive dishes like *shinsollo*. Though these rather soft-textured, yellow nuts are unique, they are nonetheless a fairly expensive delicacy.

Ginseng (*insam*): The famous anthropomorphic root of Korea, usually thought of as a medicinal plant, but also widely eaten as a rejuvenating food. Fresh young rootlets are dressed in a chilli vinegar sauce; or slices of ginseng can be eaten raw, dipped in honey. Ginseng is also added to cooked dishes, such as the popular restorative, *samgyae tang* – chicken stuffed with glutinous rice and ginseng. Though widely available in Korea, fresh ginseng may be considerably harder to come by here, if not impossible. Dried ginseng, however, is widely available, and reconstituted, may be added to cooked foods, or else boiled up into *insamcha* – ginseng tea, a potent pick-me-up.

Jujubes: Known also as Chinese dates, jujubes, like ginseng, are generally valued for their medicinal properties. They are available dried and must usually be reconstituted before use in cooking, or in Korean sweets.

Kimchi: The best *kimchi* of course is homemade, but for those who have neither the inclination nor the time to try their hand at this fermented pickle, bottled versions are available at Korean grocers and can be quite acceptable. For a Korean meal, better shop-bought *kimchi* than no *kimchi*.

Konnyaku: Jellied curd made from alimentary paste. Konnyaku has little taste but it does add superb, chewy texture to dishes such as *chongol* or *yachaesanjok*.

Korean cabbage (***paechu***): Large, oblong head of firmly-packed leaves, the essential ingredient for *kimchi*. Chinese cabbage is similar, and widely available.

Korean radish and turnip (***muu*** and ***sunmu***): Long, pointed, or large round root vegetables more similar to our turnips than to our little salad radishes. Crisp and mild in flavour, both are essential ingredients in *kimchi*, and are also enjoyed as raw salads (*muusaengchae* and *sunmunamul*). There are many different varieties in Korea, all of different sizes and shapes. Here, Chinese radish or mooli is widely available, both from oriental grocers, as well as in supermarkets.

Mushrooms (*posot*): Many varieties are enjoyed by the Koreans. Of those widely available, the most popular are dried *shiitake* mushrooms (*pyogo*); fresh *shiitake* mushrooms; dried (Chinese) mushrooms; pine mushrooms (*songi*); wood ear mushrooms (*mogi posot*); and stone mushrooms (*sogi posot*). The latter two are outstanding and are available dried from Korean grocers.

Noodles: Koreans are noodle lovers: wherever you are, a noodle stand or house is never far away. The three essential noodles to have on hand in a Korean store cupboard are *tangmyon* (made from sweet potato or mung bean flour, rather transparent and slippery in texture — essential for *chap chae* — substitute Chinese rice vermicelli); *naengmyon* (buckwheat noodles, delicious cold — substitute Japanese *soba* noodles) and *son myon* (thin wheat noodles for *kuksu* — substitute Japanese *somen* noodles).

Pine nuts: These characteristic sappy nuts, familiar enough in European kitchens, are also popular in Korea. Pine nuts are used to make gruel, ground up in Korean sweet cakes, or used as an attractive garnish.

Red chilli peppers (*kochu*); red pepper or chilli powder; red pepper threads: Red chilli peppers are an essential Korean ingredient, eaten both fresh and dried. Dried peppers are coarsely ground into powder for use as a seasoning and in making *kimchi* and they are also cut into thin threads which make an attractive garnish. Fresh Korean red peppers are similar to fresh cayenne peppers. Substitute cayenne powder or *piri piri* for Korean red pepper powder.

Journal Notes

The Importance of Being Male
I read a piece in the Korea *Times today: 'Pusan man commits suicide because of failure to sire son.' Even today, in this constantly developing country, the value placed on male children is still frighteningly high. Everywhere we go, in Seoul or in the country, women cluster around Kim and our baby Guy: 'Kochu? Kochu?' they demand, roughly prodding his nappied 'red chilli pepper' or holding up one erect finger to demonstrate. When Kim answers* ne — *yes, they beam with delight and smack her heartily on the back.*

Red pepper paste (*kochujang*): *Kochujang*, made from soy bean paste, red pepper powder and glutinous rice flour, is one of the essential seasonings of the Korean kitchen, used in stews, as an ingredient in dressings for vegetables, or as a dip. In the past, most families made their own, but bottled *kochujang* is widely available from Korean grocers and usually of good quality. Once opened it should be kept tightly covered and wrapped in a plastic bag in the refrigerator. Chinese chilli paste with garlic may be substituted.

Rice: Korean rice is a medium-grain variety that is quite sticky when cooked thus making it possible to eat with metal-pointed chopsticks. Purchase it from Korean grocers not in one- or two-pound (500 g or 1 kg bags), but by the ten or twenty-five pound (5 – 12.5 kg) sack. Japanese rice makes an adequate substitute.

Glutinous Korean rice is a short-grain variety, necessary for making Korean sweets.

Rice flour is widely used in cooking.

Rice cakes (*ttok*) are popular festive fare. They can of course be made at home, but they can also be purchased ready-made from Korean grocers.

Roasted barley: Deep-brown, roasted barley is necessary to prepare the staple tea of Korea, *poricha*, a quenching and satisfying drink either hot, lukewarm or cold.

Salted and pickled fish: Great stacks of salted and slightly salted fish are a feature of every Korean market, and indeed, this basic food forms part of the everyday diet. Dried cuttlefish (*ojingo*) remains a favourite Korean snack food (simply chewed or cooked over a flame), while salted shredded pollock strips (*pugo*) become *pugomuchim*, a ubiquitous side dish served at most meals. Dried anchovies (*marunmyolchi*) are deep-fried, then seasoned with red pepper paste, garlic, and sugar for a crunchy, delicious snack.

Salted or soused fish are also essential ingredients in making *kimchi*. Soused anchovies, available by the jar from Korean grocers, are what Halmoni generally uses to make her *kimchi*. Others prefer to use salted prawns (*saeujot*). We find that bottled anchovy essence (not necessarily of Korean origin) is a convenient substitute.

Seaweed: Seaweed and kelp are harvested the length of Korea's considerable coastline and are important features of its diet. *Miyok* is brown seaweed, used to make seaweed soup or *namul*; *kim* is pressed laver, delicious toasted with sesame oil; *tasima* is kelp, sold in thick strips. There are many other varieties available, too.

Sesame leaves (*kkaetnip*): A most delicious and interesting vegetable, eaten raw with rice and *kochujang*, or stuffed with meat and fried in batter. Fresh sesame leaves may be difficult to come by (unless you grow your own); however, tinned sesame leaves are available from Korean grocers.

Sesame oil (*chamgirum*): Another essential flavouring and seasoning of the Korean kitchen. Korean sesame oil is made from toasted sesame seeds, and thus has a characteristic robust, nutty aroma and flavour. Do note that quality in sesame oil varies considerably: choose a good, high quality brand, preferably Korean or Japanese.

Sesame seeds: White sesame seeds toasted over a flame, and crushed with salt are an important and common seasoning and garnish, used extensively. Both black and white sesame seeds are also used to make popular gruels, or as a garnish.

Soy sauce (*kanjang*): Staple flavouring and seasoning made from fermented soy bean cakes, water, and salt. Soy sauce can be either light, medium, or heavy. Halmoni has always preferred to use medium soy sauce (such as Japanese Kikkoman). Remember that soy sauce is very salty, so always taste before adding additional salt to dishes.

Soy bean paste (*twoenjang*): Another pungent and characteristic flavouring, used to make soups, sauces, and dips. *Twoenjang* is a thick brown paste made from fermented soy bean cakes, red pepper and salt. Though homemade versions can be overpowering, nonetheless it is one of the cornerstones of Korean cooking. Japanese miso is a similar bean paste product, and can be substituted if necessary.

Spring onions (*pa*): Spring onions of every size and shape are widely used in the Korean kitchen, and indeed there are numerous distinct varieties. The most common are usually somewhat larger than the spring onions we are accustomed to; also popular are both wild spring onions (tiny, more like chives in appearance and taste) and wild leeks.

Vinegar (*cho*): Rice vinegar is favoured since it is at once delicate, light and slightly sweet. Substitute, if necessary, with cider vinegar.

Watercress (*minari*): *Minari* is a particular Korean favourite, blanched and dressed as a *namul*, or used as an ingredient in soups. Its slightly bitter, peppery flavour we think is exceptional, and of course, it is widely available here.

Wine (*chu*): Korean rice wine is generally used in the kitchen for cooking. However, dry sherry makes a more than adequate substitute.

Some Basic Recipes

The following recipes are for items that are used repeatedly in Korean cooking and which are referred to in the recipes.

TOASTED SESAME SEEDS

깨소금

Toasted sesame seeds are a characteristic Korean flavouring, used as an ingredient in marinades, as well as a garnish for salads and other dishes. Make a large batch, and store in a screw-top jar.

4 oz (125 g) sesame seeds
4 teaspoons salt

Heat a frying pan to medium-hot, and add the sesame seeds. Cook, tossing and turning the seeds until they begin to brown and take on the characteristic toasted aroma. Remove before they burn and pop. Place in a mortar, together with salt, and crush with a pestle to release more aroma and flavour. Store in a screw-top jar.

CHOJANG I VINEGAR DIPPING SAUCE

초 장

Chojang is an essential condiment of the Korean table, used as a dressing for vegetables, a dip for fried fish, meats, fritters, and dumplings, or simply as a flavouring ingredient. Everybody has their own version, but do experiment to include more or less of those ingredients — chillies, chopped garlic, sesame oil, fresh coriander — whichever you like best. Here is Halmoni's recipe for making a large batch to store and use as necessary. Below, we also include two variations, made in smaller quantities.

6 tablespoons rice or cider vinegar
$\frac{3}{4}$ pint (450 ml) soy sauce
2 heaped teaspoons toasted sesame seeds
1 in (2.5 cm) piece of fresh ginger, peeled, crushed, and finely chopped
2 teaspoons red pepper powder
2 teaspoons sugar

Mix all the ingredients together and stir well. Store in a screw-top jar in the refrigerator and use as needed.

CHOJANG II SESAME VINEGAR DIPPING SAUCE

초 장

3 tablespoons soy sauce
$\frac{1}{2}$ tablespoon vinegar
1 teaspoon sesame oil
1 teaspoon sugar
1 teaspoon toasted sesame seeds
1 spring onion, finely chopped

Mix all the ingredients together and stir well. Use as a dressing for steamed vegetables, or as a dipping accompaniment.

CHOJANG III CHILLI/GARLIC VINEGAR DIPPING SAUCE

초 장

1 tablespoon rice or cider vinegar
4 tablespoons soy sauce
1 teaspoon sugar
2 teaspoons sesame oil
2 teaspoons toasted sesame seeds
Chopped fresh chillies to taste, and/or chopped garlic, and/or
chopped fresh ginger, and/or chopped fresh coriander
1 teaspoon red pepper powder

Mix all the ingredients together and stir well. Serve in saucers as a dipping accompaniment.

KOCHUJANG RED PEPPER SAUCE

고추장

Kochujang, the characteristic red pepper, bean and glutinous rice paste, is usually purchased in jars already prepared, and is an essential staple of the Korean kitchen.

However, a more tasty red pepper sauce to be served as a dip or dressing can be made by adding a few more ingredients to the already prepared basic sauce.

2 tablespoons *kochujang*
2 garlic cloves, peeled, crushed, and finely chopped
1 tablespoon rice or cider vinegar
1 tablespoon soy sauce
1 teaspoon sesame oil
2 teaspoons toasted sesame seeds
2 spring onions, shredded finely on the diagonal
2 teaspoons sugar

Mix all the ingredients together and serve in saucers as a dip, with grilled meats, raw fish, or vegetables.

VINEGAR MUSTARD SAUCE

초친 겨자

Another important basic dipping and seasoning sauce, particularly delicious with raw fish or boiled beef.

3 tablespoons soy sauce
1½ tablespoons rice or cider vinegar
1 tablespoon mustard powder or to taste

Mix all the ingredients together and place in saucers as a dipping sauce.

FRIED EGG GARNISH

계란 부침

Fresh organic eggs, bright yellow without the addition of food colouring, are fried, then cut into ribbon-thin strips to make a most attractive garnish for any number of dishes.

2 eggs
Vegetable oil for frying

The key to this simple garnish is to fry the eggs one at a time so that they are very thin. Beat each one separately by breaking into a bowl and mixing well with the hand (not with a fork, which adds too much air). Heat a large frying pan with a little vegetable oil and pour in the first egg. Spread out as thinly as possible and fry for a minute or two, then flip with a spatula. Remove, place on a board, roll up and cut into thin ribbons to use as a garnish. Repeat with the second egg. If desired, you may also separate the eggs into yolk and white to make different coloured garnishes for special decoration.

3
Anju (Appetizers)

Korean meals are not generally served in courses: rather, an enormous range of bowls, saucers, and dishes is placed on the table all at once, and you help yourself to whatever you like. (Sometimes, even rice cakes and other sweet dessert foods are presented at the same time as the savoury foods, just as, for example, in parts of rural Britain, where the meat and potatoes might be served on a farmhouse table together with an apple pie and a pile of sliced bread, butter, and jam.) The exception is at formal meals in restaurants or homes where foods may be served in succession — perhaps as many as eleven or thirteen courses — each following one after another. Only after enjoying such a leisurely feast of finely prepared foods will you be offered a bowl of rice and soup served, together perhaps, with some more spicy or fiery side dishes. The *panchan*, it is thus implied, have been so abundant that the usual filler foods, such as rice and soup, are hardly even necessary.

Appetizers, or first courses as we might consider them, generally do not fit into the Korean scheme of eating. On the other hand, Koreans are great nibblers, and one hardly goes for long in the course of a day without being offered a tempting selection of titbits, morsels, or appetizing snacks to munch on. In particular, Koreans hardly ever drink alcohol without having something to eat. Thus, in homes as well as in *sul-jip* — drinking houses — a phenomenal array of *anju* — drinking snacks — may be offered. Indeed, only in the *tapas* bars of Andalusia have we ever encountered so great and abundant an array of appetizing nibbles: savoury, pungent, or strong-flavoured foods which help promote a healthy thirst and provide a comfortable bed for copious quantities of liquor, *makkolli*, *soju*, or beer to rest upon.

If you would like to create a *chuansang* — a drinking table —

prepare these *anju* in any number or combination — the more the better — as an array to accompany drinks either throughout an evening, or before sitting down to the main meal. Or else prepare one or two foods only — *pajon*, *pindaettok*, or a platter of raw oysters — to pass around with drinks, or to eat as a first course 'haole style'.

PAJON SPRING ONION PANCAKE

파 전

Pajon is a classic: in Seoul city centre markets, at rest stops high in the mountains, or at popular venues such as the Korean Folk Village at Suwon, there will always be somebody on hand, poised over a hot, well-greased griddle, making these delicious spring onion pancakes to eat as a snack, or to accompany frothy mugs of *makkolli* or carafes of *tong dong ju*. And in Korean homes, too, this is something which everybody always loves. This recipe makes 2–3 large pancakes.

> 2 eggs, beaten together by hand
> $\frac{1}{2}$ lb (250 g) flour
> 1 tablespoon vegetable oil
> About $\frac{1}{3}$ pint (200 ml) water (enough to make a medium batter)

About 10 large spring onions or 20 small ones, split lengthwise and cut into 4 in (10 cm) pieces
1 courgette, cut into 4 in (10 cm) matchsticks
1 large carrot, peeled, and cut into 4 in (10 cm) matchsticks
$\frac{1}{4}$ lb (125 g) peeled prawns
A handful of fresh-snipped chives
4 eggs, beaten by hand
Peanut or soy oil for frying

Mix the eggs, flour, vegetable oil, and sufficient water together to make a medium batter. Allow to rest for about 15–20 minutes.

Heat a large frying pan or griddle with just enough oil to coat the bottom. Ladle enough batter to make a large, round or oblong pancake. Lay about half or a third of the spring onions, courgette and carrot matchsticks, prawns, and chives in a line on the batter.

Cook for about 5–7 minutes over a medium-hot heat. While the pancake is cooking, spoon beaten egg on to the spring onion side to fill in the gaps between the vegetables. When the egg has set and the pancake bottom is well browned, flip over. Don't worry too much if the pancake breaks up as it will be torn into small pieces before eating. Cook for a further 5−7 minutes, pressing down with a spatula to ensure that the batter cooks through.

Remove from the frying pan, drain on kitchen paper, and either serve whole to be torn up at the table, or else cut into small squares. Use remaining batter and vegetables to make one or two more pancakes.

Serve with *chojang* vinegar dipping sauce.

FAMILY-STYLE *PAJON*

파 전

This is my mother's somewhat more substantial version of *pajon*. It is a great favourite of ours, delicious eaten hot off the griddle, or else cold as a snack. It is a deceptively simple recipe that always works.

3 large eggs, beaten
4 oz (125 g) plain flour

$\frac{1}{2}$ lb (250 g) steak (rump or sirloin)
2 tablespoons soy sauce
$\frac{1}{2}$ tablespoon sesame oil
1 clove garlic, peeled, crushed and finely chopped
$\frac{1}{2}$ in (12 mm) piece of fresh ginger, peeled, crushed, and finely chopped
$\frac{1}{2}$ teaspoon toasted sesame seeds
Freshly ground black pepper

About 15−20 spring onions, cut into 2−3 in (5−7.5 cm) pieces (if large, then split first)
3 stalks of celery, cut into thin strips length-wise, then into 3 in (7.5 cm) pieces
1 tablespoon salt
2 oz (50 g) cabbage *kimchi*, rinsed and sliced (optional)
2 fresh chillies, seeded and coarsely chopped

Vegetable oil for frying

In a large mixing bowl, add the flour to the beaten eggs and mix well to make a stiff paste.

Marinade the meat with the soy sauce, sesame oil, garlic, ginger, sesame seeds, and black pepper. Sprinkle the celery with the salt, and add water to cover. Soak for 15 minutes or until limp, then rinse, drain, and squeeze dry. Add the prepared vegetables, *kimchi* if using, and the marinaded meat to the paste and mix well with the hands (the paste may seem rather stiff, but the water in the vegetables and meat will thin it).

Heat a large frying pan over a medium flame, and add sufficient vegetable oil for frying. When hot, ladle large spoonfuls of the meat and vegetable paste into the pan and fry until brown and cooked through, about 5−7 minutes or so, pressing down with a spatula to flatten. Turn and fry on the other side for a further 5 minutes. Drain on kitchen paper, and continue until all the mixture is cooked into fritters. Slice into 2 in (5 cm) squares, and arrange on a platter.

Serve immediately or at room temperature with *chojang* vinegar dipping sauce.

YUKHOE KOREAN STEAK TARTARE

육 회

As a child, I was always sneaking pieces of raw beef − *pulgogi* meat − which my mother was marinading for that night's dinner. I didn't know it at the time, but I was indulging in a Korean favourite: *yukhoe*, far more delicious than steak tartare.

Today, when Halmoni makes this speciality, she insists on organically reared meat that she knows contains no harmful additives or hormones (we ourselves are also great believers in organic meat and poultry). Traditionally, says Halmoni, *yukhoe* is eaten as a chaser when drinking wine or *soju*. For those timid souls who do not like eating raw meat, spoon it over hot steamed rice to cook it very slightly.

1 lb (500 g) rump steak (superior cuts such as sirloin or fillet, says Halmoni, give too soft a texture)

---

3 tablespoons soy sauce
1 tablespoon sesame oil
2 garlic cloves, peeled, crushed, and finely chopped
$\frac{1}{2}$ in (12 mm) piece of fresh ginger, peeled, crushed, and finely chopped
1 heaped tablespoon sugar
1 tablespoon rice wine or dry sherry
1 tablespoon toasted sesame seeds
Plenty of freshly ground black pepper

---

1 Korean pear, peeled, cored, and sliced into thin matchsticks
1 teaspoon sugar
2 large spring onions, finely shredded on the diagonal
1 teaspoon toasted sesame seeds

The key to making *yukhoe* lies in the slicing. It is essential first to trim the meat of every scrap of gristle, fat, or sinew. Then slice the meat extremely thinly across the grain into slices, then cut these slices into the thinnest matchstick strips possible. Mix the marinade ingredients together and add to the meat. Mix well with the hands, form into a loose ball, and chill in the refrigerator for an hour or two until serving.

Meanwhile, soak the thin Korean pear strips in a bowl of water together with the teaspoon of sugar for 5 minutes. Drain and arrange the pear strips decoratively on a dish, coming out from the centre like spokes to form a circular pattern. Place the meat, still in a loosely formed ball, on top of the pear strips, and garnish with the shredded spring onions and toasted sesame seeds.

SAMGYOPSALGUI GRILLED BELLY PORK

삼겹살구이

Rolled sides of belly pork — uncured bacon — are popular in the *suljip* drinking houses of Seoul, Pusan, and elsewhere: the somewhat fatty meat is cut into thin slices and a platter of this is given to drinkers to cook themselves over a tabletop burner. Afterwards, the charred, slightly burnt pieces are dipped in a simple mixture of sesame oil and salt: the sort of snack to help you work up a decent thirst!

1 lb (500 g) belly pork
4 tablespoons sesame oil
2 teaspoons sea salt

Buy the belly pork in a single piece and cut the slices yourself: about $\frac{1}{8}$ in (3 mm) thick. Cook over a tabletop burner, a charcoal fire, or under a grill, until crispy and cooked through. Drain on kitchen paper, arrange on a platter, and eat while piping hot, dipped into the sesame oil and sea salt mixed together.

YACHAESANJOK VEGETABLE AND MEAT FRITTERS

야채산적

This is Halmoni's very special and elaborate variation of the more often encountered *pajon*: spring onions, other vegetables, and meat laid out in strips, threaded onto skewers, dipped in flour and egg, and fried. It is refined palace food; certainly it is a lot of work to make, but the result really is superlative. This recipe makes a large platter to pass around with drinks or to serve as a first course.

30 large spring onions, cut into 4 in (10 cm) pieces
1 teaspoon salt
2 teaspoons toasted sesame seeds

---

5 stalks celery
2 tablespoons salt

---

2 lb (1 kg) sirloin steak, cut across the grain into thin 3 in (7.5 cm) strips
1 tablespoon soy sauce
2 teaspoons sesame oil
1 teaspoon toasted sesame seeds
1 clove garlic, peeled, crushed, and finely chopped
$\frac{1}{2}$ in (12 mm) piece of fresh ginger, peeled, crushed, and finely chopped

---

1 cake *konnyaku*, cut into 3 in (7.5 cm) strips
2 teaspoons toasted sesame seeds
1 tablespoon soy sauce
$\frac{1}{2}$ tablespoon sesame oil

About 4 oz (125 g) cabbage *kimchi*, rinsed, and cut into even 3 in (7.5 cm) lengths.

6–8 eggs
$\frac{1}{2}$ lb (250 g) flour
Vegetable oil for frying
About 15 wooden skewers

Place the cut spring onions in a bowl and mix well with the salt and toasted sesame seeds. String the stalks of celery, cut lengthwise into thin strips, then into pieces about 3 inches (7.5 cm) long. Place in a bowl together with the salt, cover with water, and leave for about 15 minutes or until limp. Rinse, drain and squeeze dry. Marinade the sliced steak in the marinade ingredients. Mix the *konnyaku* strips with the soy sauce, sesame oil, and toasted sesame seeds.

Take the wooden skewers and thread each through the top of a spring onion, then a piece of *kimchi*, then a strip of celery, then a strip of marinaded steak, then a piece of *konnyaku*, and finally another spring onion, and pieces of *kimchi*, celery, steak, and *konnyaku* again. Lay the skewers out neatly and flat in a large dish and continue until all the ingredients have been used.

Break the eggs into a flat rectangular dish, and mix well with the hands. Spread out the flour in another flat dish. Heat vegetable oil in a large frying pan to medium-hot. Lay each skewer first in the flour, pressing down on both sides, then dip into the beaten eggs, coating well. Place one at a time in the hot frying pan, laid out flat. Fry until brown, about 5−7 minutes. While cooking, spoon over some more beaten egg to fill in the gaps between the vegetable and meat strips. Turn and cook another 5 minutes or so on the other side until brown. Remove and drain on kitchen paper.

Continue frying all the remaining skewers. When they have all drained on kitchen paper, remove the skewers, and cut each into 2 in (5 cm) squares. Serve with *chojang* vinegar dipping sauce.

Korean Folk Village

The Korean Folk Village, located at Suwon, about an hour's drive south of Seoul, is a remarkable replica of a typical nineteenth-century Yi dynasty Korean village, consisting of over two hundred and fifty reconstructed houses, buildings, workshops and craft-shops. As such, it provides a fascinating insight into traditional architecture as well as into the social structure and ways of living in a highly stratified society. There are replicas of a thatched house from Kyonsangbuk-do; large farmers' dwellings; *yangban* mansions; a provincial governor's dwelling; private schools and academies; a Chinese herb medicine dispensary; a Buddhist temple; and a marketplace where traditional crafts such as wooden masks, brassware, willow and bambooware, and mulberry paper are all made by hand. In this central area, you can take your shoes off and sit on raised platforms under waving canvas awnings and enjoy carafes of sensational *tong dong ju* (farmers' rice wine) together with drinking snacks like *pindaettok*, *pajon*, *totori muk*, and much else.

KUJOLPAN NINE-SECTION APPETIZER

구 절판

Kujolpan is a classic: a selection of foods served in an elegant octagonal lacquerware dish that holds pancakes in the middle compartment. Each diner (or drinker) selects a homemade pancake and adds whatever stuffing he or she desires — a bit of meat, some cucumber or carrot strips, egg, mushrooms, or prawns — then rolls it up to eat with the fingers. Though undoubtedly part of the appeal of this dish is its beautiful receptacle, you can of course arrange the ingredients attractively on a large plate, with the pile of pancakes in the middle.

4 oz (125 g) flour
About $\frac{1}{3}$ pint (200 ml) water
1 teaspoon salt

$\frac{1}{4}$ lb (125 g) sirloin steak, trimmed and cut into very fine strips
1 tablespoon soy sauce
$\frac{1}{2}$ tablespoon sesame oil
1 teaspoon toasted sesame seeds
1 garlic clove, peeled, crushed, and finely chopped
1 spring onion, finely chopped
1 teaspoon sugar
Freshly ground black pepper

$\frac{1}{2}$ cucumber
1 teaspoon salt
1 teaspoon sesame oil

---

1 carrot
1 teaspoon sugar
1 teaspoon rice or cider vinegar
$\frac{1}{2}$ teaspoon red pepper powder

$\frac{1}{4}$ lb (125 g) bamboo shoots
$\frac{1}{2}$ in (12 mm) piece of fresh ginger, peeled, crushed, and finely chopped
1 teaspoon soy sauce
1 teaspoon sesame oil

$\frac{1}{4}$ lb (125 g) small peeled prawns
$\frac{1}{2}$ teaspoon sugar
1 teaspoon rice or cider vinegar

---

6 dried mushrooms, washed, trimmed, and soaked for 3–4 hours
1 teaspoon soy sauce

½ teaspoon sugar
1 teaspoon sesame oil

---

2 eggs, separated into white and yolk, beaten by hand

Make the pancakes first: mix the flour together with sufficient water and a pinch of salt to make a smooth batter. Set aside for 1 hour. Then, in a hot lightly oiled frying pan, drop in tablespoons of batter to make thin pancakes about 3 in (7.5 cm) in diameter. Fry lightly on both sides. Set aside in piles.

Prepare the fillings next. Mix the thinly sliced steak with the seasonings, and stir-fry for about 5 minutes or until cooked.

Cut the cucumber into thin matchsticks and sprinkle with salt. Set aside for 15 minutes, then rinse and squeeze dry. Stir-fry in sesame oil for about 2−3 minutes. Cut the carrot into very thin matchsticks and dress with sugar, vinegar, and red pepper powder. Cut the bamboo shoots into thin matchsticks, mix with ginger and soy sauce, and stir-fry in sesame oil for 2−3 minutes. Slice the prawns into thin strips and dress with sugar and vinegar.

Drain the soaked mushrooms and cut into thin strips. Mix with the seasonings and stir-fry gently until tender, about 8−10 minutes.

Fry the separated beaten egg yolk and egg whites separately in thin sheets, then slice into thin 2 in (5 cm) strips, so that you end up with a pile of white strips and a pile of yellow ones.

To assemble, place the pile of pancakes in the centre of the *kujolpan* dish or in the centre of a large, attractive platter. Arrange the 8 ingredients around the pancakes. To eat, simply take a pancake and fill it with any combination of fillings to taste.

The Life of a *Yangban*
My grandmother's grandfather, my great-great-grandfather, was a high-ranking *yangban* official for the last Yi dynasty king. As Provincial Governor of the Chungchong province of central Korea, his family was very wealthy, remembers Halmoni, and they lived in a large house, with both servants and slaves to look after them. (Slavery was not abolished until the reforms of 1894.)

He must have cut a splendid figure, my great-great-grandfather, in his official dark-blue uniform embroidered with the design of a crane, for such high-ranking officials wore their imposing official dress even at home. At court, they wore even grander red or blue silks likewise embroidered with patterns, decorative belts, and striking crown-shaped hats made of woven horse-hair.

At home, great-great-grandfather had his own *sarangbang* or living area, a master's quarter that consisted, probably, of at least three rooms where he would retire to study, compose poetry, practise calligraphy, and drink wine with his men friends. This inner sanctum would have been simply furnished with bookshelves, a writing table, a table for his inkstone, stands for the writing brushes and for his long bamboo smoking pipes. Women — except for favoured *kisaengs*, skilled in the arts of music, poetry, painting, and love — were rarely allowed to enter into such a male preserve.

KIMGUI FLAME-ROASTED LAVER

김구이

Sheets of pressed laver, painted with sesame oil, and roasted over an open flame, are a great *yangban* favourite, says Halmoni. Make a pile to serve as a crispy 'chaser' with drinks; or serve as a side dish; or use as a garnish for *pibimpab* and other dishes.

$\frac{1}{2}$ **packet of *kim* (pressed laver); about 10 sheets**
$4\frac{1}{2}$ **tablespoons sesame oil**
$\frac{1}{2}$ **teaspoon salt**
Toasted sesame seeds

Separate the sheets of pressed laver. Mix together the sesame oil and salt. Paint each side of each sheet with the salted oil, stack together and wrap up in cling film. Leave for about 30 minutes.

On a gas fire, pass the sheets of laver over the flame one at a time, holding them with tongs, until crispy. Alternatively lay each sheet in a hot frying pan until crispy. When done, sprinkle with toasted sesame seeds, and cut into small squares or strips.

KIMBAP STUFFED LAVER AND RICE ROLLS

김밥

This Korean 'street food' makes a delicious picnic food, snack, or appetizer. Koreans use bamboo string rollers to wrap the rolls, making the task considerably easier.

About 8 sheets of laver, lightly toasted
4–6 oz (125–175 g) cooked white rice
3 tablespoons rice or cider vinegar
3 eggs, beaten, fried, and cut into thin strips
½ lb (250 g) spinach, steamed and chopped coarsely
2 teaspoons sesame oil
1 teaspoon toasted sesame seeds
1 carrot, peeled and cut into matchsticks
¼ lb (125 g) cooked beef, pork, or ham, cut into matchstick slivers

Lay the lightly toasted laver sheets out on a board. Spread each with cooked rice, and sprinkle with the vinegar. Mix the spinach with the sesame oil and toasted sesame seeds. Spread the egg strips, dressed spinach, carrot matchsticks, and slivers of meat over the rice lengthwise. Carefully and tightly roll up lengthwise. Slice into small bite-sized rolls.

TASIMA DEEP-FRIED KELP

튀 각

Thick, dried pieces of brown kelp (*tasima*) are another Korean drinking snack, delicious — crispy and chewy at the same time — fried in sesame oil and sprinkled with sugar.

1 packet *tasima* (2–4 oz/50–125 g)
Vegetable oil for deep-frying (about ½ pt/300 ml)
2 tablespoons sesame oil
1 tablespoon sugar for sprinkling

Cut each length of *tasima* into pieces about 1½ inches (3.5 cm) long. Heat the vegetable oil and sesame oil together in a large pot for deep-frying. When the oil reaches a medium-hot temperature (before it is smoking), add the pieces of *tasima* and fry for only 10 seconds or so, until the surface crackles and bubbles up. Take care not to let it burn. Remove and drain on kitchen paper. Sprinkle with sugar.

KEJON FRIED CRAB CAKES

게 전

These fried crab cakes are a typical Korean *anju*. They can be nibbled while drinking, or else served as part of a Korean meal.

White meat from 2 cooked crabs, shredded
3 spring onions, finely chopped
1 in (2.5 cm) piece of fresh root ginger, peeled, crushed, and finely chopped
1 teaspoon toasted sesame seeds
2 eggs, beaten
1 tablespoon flour
1 teaspoon salt
2 tablespoons fresh coriander, chopped

3 tablespoons flour for dredging
Vegetable oil for frying

Place the shredded crab meat in a mixing bowl and add the chopped spring onions, ginger, toasted sesame seeds, beaten eggs, flour, salt, and chopped fresh coriander. Mix well, then form into small flat cakes. Dredge the cakes in flour.

Heat vegetable oil in a frying pan, and when medium-hot, shallowfry the crab cakes for about 5−7 minutes each side or until brown and cooked through. Drain on kitchen towel. Serve immediately, together with saucers of *chojang* vinegar dipping sauce.

Lacquerware
The art of lacquerware has been 'practised in Korea since the days of the Koryo dynasty (AD 927−1392), and indeed today a great variety of beautiful objects are still made.

Originally, numerous materials were used as inlays − tortoiseshell, mother-of-pearl, horn, bone, silver and copper thread, and brass − then the objects were coloured (usually either red or black) and finally highly polished with several coats of lacquer.

In the Yi dynasty period, however, simpler designs mainly utilizing mother-of-pearl predominated, depicting such classic motifs as the plum, bamboo, orchid and chrysanthemum, as well as other stylized longevity symbols.

CLAM CAKES

대합구이

There are scores of different types of clams gathered and enjoyed all around the Korean coast. These delicious clam cakes can be made with whatever sort are available.

1 pound chopped clams with their liquid
3—4 fresh chillies, finely chopped
1 small onion, peeled, and finely chopped
1 bunch fresh coriander or parsley, chopped
About 4 oz (125 g) flour (use more or less depending on the amount
of clam liquid)
1 teaspoon salt
1 teaspoon baking soda
1 egg

Vegetable oil for frying

Mix the ingredients together to make a rather stiff but workable batter. Heat vegetable oil in a frying pan, and fry spoonfuls of the mixture, pressing down to make flat cakes, about 5—7 minutes a side. Drain on kitchen paper, and serve with *chojang* vinegar dipping sauce.

Journal Notes

Street Food

Everywhere we go, we see stalls offering great cauldrons of steamed mussels for passersby to prise off their half-shells together with a nip of throat-burning soju. There are stands selling noodles in soup served, of course, with saucers of kimchi. *There are plates of chewy, rubbery ttok — rice cakes in a deep red chilli sauce. Elsewhere, women fry Korean pancakes —* pajon *and* pindaettok *— on well-greased griddles while thin strips of sweet potatoes are deep-fried like fine french fries. And there are charcoal braziers on every corner, roasting chestnuts or grilling* ojingo *— flattened, dusty cuttlefish or squid — a chewy, salty food.*

At dusk, tents mysteriously appear on every street corner, their inner tables loaded with an amazing range of raw shellfish and fish, morsels of grilled meat and liver, fried food, seaweed, kimchi, *and much else — all food which helps work up a powerful thirst. The canvas walls of these literally fly-by-night establishments reverberate from the sounds of singing and the raucous clanging of metal chopsticks well into the small hours as white-collar workers, who just 'happened to be passing by', enjoy another long night of revelry.*

KULWIGIM DEEP-FRIED OYSTERS

굴튀김

**24 oysters, opened
Salt
Freshly ground black pepper
4 oz (125 g) flour
1 egg
2 teaspoons baking powder
4 tablespoons water
Oil for deep-frying**

Season the washed and opened oysters with salt and black pepper. Beat the flour, egg, baking powder, and water together to make a batter.

Heat a pan about half full with vegetable oil for deep-frying. Dip the oysters in the batter and deep-fry for 3—5 minutes or until the batter is crisp and brown. Do not overcook. The oysters should still be succulent and juicy inside. Drain on kitchen paper and serve with *chojang* vinegar dipping sauce.

PINDAETTOK MUNG BEAN PANCAKE

빈 대떡

Pindaettok is another classic drinking snack, delicious served straight off the hot griddle. Many restaurants call this speciality 'Korean pizza' but it really is nothing at all like that Italian stand-by.

$\frac{1}{2}$lb (250 g) dried mung beans
2 oz (50 g) rice

2 oz (50 g) lean pork
1 garlic clove, peeled, crushed, and finely chopped
$\frac{1}{4}$in (6 mm) piece of fresh ginger, peeled, crushed, and finely chopped
$\frac{1}{2}$ teaspoon sesame oil
Freshly ground black pepper

3 spring onions, shredded on the diagonal
1–2 red chillies, seeded and cut into very thin strips
Handful of fresh coriander, coarsely chopped

Vegetable oil for frying

Soak the mung beans in warm water for 3 hours. Soak the rice separately for the same time. Rinse both separately in several changes of fresh water. Rub the skins off the beans and discard. Grind the beans and rice together in a blender or food processor with about $\frac{1}{4}$pint (150 ml) water until a fairly thick paste is formed.

Slice the pork into thin strips, and mix together with the garlic, ginger, sesame oil, and pepper. Set aside to marinade for 1 hour.

To cook, heat some vegetable oil in a large frying pan. Drop spoonfuls of the batter into the hot frying pan to fry. As the batter sets, top with strips of marinaded pork, shredded spring onion, strips of chilli, and chopped coriander. Fry for about 5 minutes, then turn and cook the other side until brown and crispy.

Drain on kitchen paper, and serve with *chojang* vinegar dipping sauce.

KKAETNIPKOGIJON STUFFED SESAME LEAVES

깻잎고기전

Sesame leaves are one of the most distinctive and delicious Korean vegetables, eaten fresh and simply seasoned with a little soy sauce, garlic, and spring onions; used as a roll-up for *pulgogi* and rice; deep-fried like seaweed; or in this case, stuffed with a tasty meat filling, dipped in flour and egg, and pan-fried. While fresh sesame leaves may be difficult to obtain (unless you grow your own), tinned ones should be available.

About 30 sesame leaves

$\frac{1}{2}$ lb (250 g) lean ground beef
2 tablespoons soy sauce
2 spring onions, finely chopped
2 garlic cloves, peeled, crushed, and finely chopped
$\frac{1}{2}$ in (12 mm) piece of fresh ginger, peeled, crushed, and finely chopped
1 tablespoon sesame oil
2 teaspoons toasted sesame seeds
Freshly ground black pepper

4 tablespoons flour
1–2 eggs, beaten

Vegetable oil for frying

Wash and pat dry the sesame leaves. Mix together the ground beef and the seasonings. Spread a spoonful of the meat mixture on to each sesame leaf, and wrap. Dip the leaves first in flour, then in beaten egg. Fry in hot oil for 5 minutes a side or until brown and crispy. Drain on kitchen paper. Serve with *chojang* vinegar soy sauce.

TAEHAP-TCHIM STEAMED STUFFED CLAMS

대합찜

Steamed clams on the half shell, swimming in a pungent mixture of soy sauce, garlic, spring onions, and sesame oil, are the sort of *anju* that are happily devoured by the dozen in countless drinking tents in Seoul, Pusan, and all along the coast. Choose small and very fresh clams.

> **2 pints (1 litre) clams in the shell**
> **3 tablespoons soy sauce**
> **1 tablespoon sesame oil**
> **2 garlic cloves, peeled, crushed, and finely chopped**
> **2 spring onions, finely chopped**
> **1 tablespoon toasted sesame seeds**
> **1 teaspoon sugar**
> **1 chilli, seeded and finely chopped**

Scrub the shells of the clams, then leave to soak overnight in a bucket of salt water so that they expel any sand or grit. Discard any clams that don't close when you give them a sharp tap.

In a large pot heat salted water to boiling, then drop in the clams and steam until they open, about 3−5 minutes. Remove from the pot, and take off one side of the shells. Loosen the clam meat from the shell, and, if large, cut into 2 or 3 pieces. Mix the remaining ingredients together, and pour a little of this sauce into each shell. Arrange on a platter and serve at once.

KULHOE RAW OYSTERS

굴 회

I love raw oysters − and indeed, we have travelled a long way to enjoy them − by the dozen at Cancale, Galway, Marennes, Colchester, Acapulco, and Haeundae Beach near Pusan. There is something so sea-fresh and invigorating about raw oysters on the half-shell, opened only just before eating, the sea-green fringe shimmering against the bright mother-of-pearl. It goes without saying, of course, that raw oysters must be impeccably fresh, indeed alive, and that the waters that they have been raised in must be free of pollution, so it is essential to know your source. Korean oysters are the Pacific *gigas* variety that are widely available here. I think they are best with no addition whatsoever, but for those who like to gild gold, we include a hot red pepper sauce. Opening oysters calls for strong hands and patience.

12–24 live oysters in the shell
Bed of fresh seaweed
Crushed ice

---

1 tablespoon *kochujang*
1 tablespoon vinegar
$\frac{1}{2}$ tablespoon sugar
$\frac{1}{2}$in (12 mm) piece of fresh ginger, peeled, crushed, and finely chopped

Wash the oysters to remove any grit or dirt from the shells. Open by inserting a strong-bladed knife between the two shells by the muscle of the hinge, then gently wriggle and prise apart. Be careful, as the oyster opens, that you don't lose the delicious juices. Discard those oysters that are already open, or which don't smell impeccably fresh. Remove the top shell and loosen the oyster by cutting it free. Open all the oysters, and arrange them on a bed of seaweed and crushed ice.

Mix together the sauce ingredients and serve in saucers. To eat, either suck the oyster directly off its shell (together with the juices), or else first spoon a little of the sauce onto each oyster.

SORA-TCHIM STUFFED STEAMED WHELKS

소라찜

Steamed whelks are generally rather tough and rubbery, but I have always enjoyed them nonetheless, in Essex simply with malt vinegar, in France dipped in garlic mayonnaise. However, the best I have ever eaten were served at a little *saengsonhoejib* near Haeundae Beach, where they were chopped and mixed with seasonings, stuffed back into their snail-like shells, laid on a bed of salt, and flambéed in *soju*. This was a most delicious nibble to whet the appetite, while waiting for the raw fish.

12 steamed whelks in the shell
1 tablespoon *kochujang*
1 garlic clove, peeled, crushed, and finely chopped
$\frac{1}{2}$in (12 mm) piece of fresh ginger, peeled, crushed, and finely chopped
2 spring onions, finely chopped
$\frac{1}{2}$ tablespoon sesame oil

About 4 tablespoons *soju* or vodka
1 cup coarse sea salt

Remove the cooked meat from the whelk shells and roughly chop. Wash the shells and set aside. Mix the whelk meat together with the *kochujang*, garlic, ginger, spring onions, sesame oil, and about 1 tablespoon of *soju* or vodka. Stuff back into the cleaned shells. Arrange them on a platter on a bed of coarse salt. Before serving, heat up the remaining *soju* or vodka in a ladle, ignite with a match, and pour over the shells to flambé.

MARUNMYOLCHI DRIED ANCHOVY APPETIZER

마른 멸치

To the uninitiated, these dried small-fry anchovies may not appear the most appetizing of dishes. But believe me, deep-fried until crispy, then coated in a hot and sweet sauce, they are delicious, a savoury, salty snack that keeps you coming back for more *maekchu*, *tong dong chu*, cold beer, or iced water. Though the amount of sugar in the sauce may seem excessive, when combined with the salt of the fish and the fire of the *kochujang*, it is just right.

1 packet dried anchovies (about 4 oz/125 g)
2 tablespoons *kochujang*
1 garlic clove, peeled, crushed, and finely chopped
4 tablespoons sugar

Oil for deep-frying

Heat a large heavy pot with sufficient oil for deep frying. When hot, add the packet of dried anchovies to the oil and fry for about 20–30 seconds, or until very crispy but not burnt. Drain with a slotted spoon, and place on kitchen paper. Drain the hot oil and reserve if desired (it can be used again for preparation of this or other fish dishes).

Mix together the *kochujang*, garlic and sugar. Return the fried anchovies to the pot, add this sauce mixture, stir well taking care not to break up the fish but ensuring that they are evenly coated, and allow to cook over a medium flame for 1 or 2 minutes. Spoon into a bowl and serve hot or cold as a nibbling snack.

MUK MUNG BEAN OR ACORN CURD WITH SOY SAUCE AND SPRING ONIONS

묵

There is a large oak tree in front of our house in Cambridge, and Uncle Donald is always wishing that we would gather the acorns and make a vegetable curd from them: for he is sorely missing his drinking *anju* which he so enjoyed during his raucous days (and nights) in Seoul. In fact, acorn and other vegetable curds may be available from Korean grocers and are ready to eat. These jelly-like slabs are really rather bland in taste, but the chewy texture combines quite marvellously with the simple sauce ingredients.

1 cake mung bean curd or acorn curd

---

3 tablespoons soy sauce
3 spring onions, very finely chopped
1 tablespoon sesame oil
$\frac{1}{2}$ teaspoon sugar

---

2 teaspoons toasted sesame seeds
6 chives, snipped in 1in (2.5 cm) pieces

Slice the mung bean or acorn curd into thin, even slices and arrange on a platter in an overlap. Mix together the sauce ingredients and pour over the curd. Leave for 30 minutes or so. Garnish with the toasted sesame seeds and snipped chives before serving.

4
Soups, Stews and One-pot Meals

Soup, glorious soup. No Korean meal is complete without it, whether it is simply a bowl of soy bean sprouts swimming in a subtle broth, a pungent *twoenjang*-flavoured medley of vegetables and clams, or a fiery, fishy and substantial Korean version of *bouillabaisse*, the classic chilli-tinted *maeuntang*. For soup, together with rice and *kimchi*, is a basic item in every Korean meal — indeed, these three form *the* basic Korean meal — anything else, any other side dish or *panchan*, is a bonus, delicious perhaps but not strictly necessary.

Most of the following soups are surprisingly simple to prepare and should be sampled not as special dishes in their own right, but as one element of a Korean meal. Others, however, are considerably more substantial, hearty one-pot meals in themselves.

Chongol and *tchigae* are not really soups at all; rather, they are soupy stews: mixtures of meat, vegetables, bean curd, or seafood cooked and served in lesser amounts of liquid, dipped into and eaten out of communal pots, not individual bowls. They are outstanding examples of Korean food at its best, balancing and preserving the integrity of individual ingredients, yet at the same time savoury and full of flavour.

KONGGUK SOY BEAN SPROUT SOUP

콩 국

A bowl of rather thin but tasty broth, floating with soy bean sprouts, is a common accompaniment to any Korean meal. Soy bean sprouts have far more flavour than more common mung bean sprouts. Buy them from Korean grocers, or else sprout your own.

~57~

$\frac{1}{2}$lb (250 g) soy bean sprouts
2 garlic cloves, peeled, crushed, and finely chopped
2 tablespoons soy sauce
2 teaspoons sesame oil
Salt
2 spring onions, shredded on the diagonal
Pinch of red pepper threads

Remove the hairlike roots from the soy bean sprouts and wash well. Steam for 5—10 minutes, then in the same pot, add the garlic, soy sauce, sesame oil, and a little salt to taste. Add about 1$\frac{1}{2}$ pints (900 ml) of water and bring to the boil. Reduce to a simmer and cook for 15 minutes. Garnish with spring onions and red pepper threads.

Journal Notes

Auntie's Seaweed for Kim
Arrived in Pusan today, and finally had the chance to meet Bong Tae's mother, our Great Aunt. Some fifty years earlier, when Halmoni was busy with her business interests in Honolulu, she had sent my mother — then a baby of only eighteen months — and my mother's brother, John, to Korea where they were brought up by this kind, now elderly woman. Great Auntie was the sister of another picture bride whom Halmoni had met on the boat to Hawaii. There they became fast and close friends, and they cemented this friendship by arranging for Halmoni's brother to meet Halmoni's friend's sister. As hoped for, the couple eventually married.

Great Auntie, who was enchanted with our little son Guy, her great nephew, gave Kim three packets of best quality Pusan seaweed, to be made, she instructed, into miyokguk — *seaweed soup* — *the traditional mainstay of nursing mothers.*

MIYOKGUK SEAWEED SOUP

미역국

Seaweed soup is not only enjoyed by nursing mothers: indeed it is a staple favourite that is eaten regularly. Uncle Larry remembers

Halmoni's *miyokguk*, simmered in a large pot, smelling of the sea, and delicious with lots of hot steamed white rice.

$\frac{1}{2}$ packet brown seaweed (*miyok*), about 2 oz (50 g)
$\frac{1}{2}$ lb (250 g) finely chopped beef
4 garlic cloves, peeled, crushed, and finely chopped
2 tablespoons sesame oil
4 tablespoons soy sauce
Water
2 spring onions, cut into 2 in (5 cm) lengths
Salt
Freshly ground black pepper
1 spring onion, shredded on the diagonal

Wash the seaweed thoroughly in a colander under running water, agitating well with the hands, then drain. Mix the finely chopped beef with the garlic, sesame oil, and soy sauce. Heat a little oil in a large pot, and fry the meat until brown. Add the drained seaweed and fry quickly for a minute or two. Pour over about 3 pints ($1\frac{1}{2}$ litres) of water and add the lengths of spring onions. Bring to the boil and simmer for an hour or until the seaweed is tender. Season with salt and plenty of freshly ground black pepper. Before serving, garnish with shredded spring onions.

CHOGAETANG CLAM SOUP

조 개탕

Another exceedingly simple everyday soup, made with numerous varieties of clams harvested around the Korean coast. Use whatever is both available and exceedingly fresh. If you live by the coast, why not do as the Koreans and gather your own?

About 2 or 3 dozen unopened clams
1 tablespoon sesame oil
1 tablespoon *twoenjang* (soy bean paste)
6 spring onions, sliced
Water
Salt
Freshly ground black pepper
2 spring onions, shredded on the diagonal

Scrub the clams and wash in several changes of water. Leave to soak overnight in a pot of salted water together with a handful of bran: this plumps up the shellfish and helps expel any sand.

Heat the sesame oil in a pot and throw in the scrubbed and soaked clams. Toss the clams in the oil, then add the *twoenjang*, spring onions, and about 1½ pints (900 ml) of water. Mix well and season with salt and freshly ground black pepper. Bring to the boil, then reduce to a simmer and cook until all the shells have opened — for about 10 minutes. Garnish with shredded spring onions and serve in individual soup bowls.

Music and Dance

That music is important to the Koreans is evident to any visitor. Walk through Seoul of an evening, and the sound of clanging chopsticks, and hearty — if somewhat tipsy — voices emerges from the hundreds of *soju* tents and *sul-jib* found on every street corner. In the mountains of Sorak-san, groups of young people sit in a circle on the rocks or at a resting place below a waterfall, clapping their hands in unison as they sing together. On Taehang-no — College Street — on a Sunday, students don long-ribboned hats to twirl wildly and acrobatically for impromptu performances of the farmer's dance, while others sit cross-legged on the ground, banging the *changgu* — hourglass drum — to appreciative, nodding listeners. Concerts of Korean classical and folk music take place regularly in the impressive Sejong Cultural Centre, while in venues such as Korea House and elsewhere there are regular nightly performances of folk and formal music.

Pansori is a particularly vivid and distinctive national form, a mixture of music, drama and verse, wherein stories are unfolded and acted out by a solo performer (known as a *kwangdae*) accompanied only by a drum. The stories in themselves are not of foremost importance since they are familiar tales which have been told and retold. Rather, it is the manner in which they are recounted — a one-person operatic performance which tests the enormous range of expressive vocal dexterity, nuances of interpretation and variations within the story structure, skills of song and mime, and musical excellence — that together determine the virtuosity of the *kwangdae*.

PAEKSUK CHICKEN SOUP

백 숙

This simple chicken soup is delicious on its own, or else as a base for noodles or *mandu*.

1 whole chicken, cleaned
3 garlic cloves, peeled
1 in (2.5 cm) piece of fresh ginger, peeled and sliced
Salt
Freshly ground black pepper
4 spring onions, sliced
1 egg, beaten, fried, and cut into strips

Place the whole chicken in a large pot and cover with water. Add the whole cloves of garlic and the sliced ginger, and season with salt and freshly ground black pepper. Bring to the boil and skim off the froth. Cover, reduce the heat, and simmer for about 1 hour. When tender, remove the chicken, discard the skin and bones, and shred the meat.

Pour the broth into bowls. Add some shredded meat to each bowl, and garnish with sliced spring onions and egg strips.

KOGIDUBUGUK BEEF AND BEAN CURD SOUP

고기두부국

Basic and bracing beef and bean curd soup, a substantial stand-by for long Korean winters.

$\frac{1}{2}$ lb (250 g) steak, sliced into thin strips
2 tablespoons soy sauce
3 spring onions, chopped
2 garlic cloves, peeled, crushed, and finely chopped
1 teaspoon toasted sesame seeds
1 tablespoon sesame oil
Water
2 cakes bean curd, cut into cubes
Salt
Freshly ground back pepper
2 spring onions, shredded on the diagonal

Place the thinly sliced steak in a bowl. Mix together the soy sauce, spring onions, garlic, toasted sesame seeds, and sesame oil, and pour over the meat. Leave to marinade for 30 minutes.

Heat a little vegetable oil in a large pot, and fry the meat until brown. Add about 2 pints (1.2 litres) of water, bring to the boil, then reduce to a simmer. Cook for 15 minutes, then add the bean curd and simmer for a further 5 minutes. Season with salt and more pepper to taste and garnish with spring onions before serving.

KALBITANG BEEF RIB SOUP

갈비탕

This hearty beef rib soup is a real favourite. The key to a good, rich-tasting *kalbitang*, says Halmoni, is to score and marinade the meat, then fry it first before adding the liquid.

$1\frac{1}{2}$lb (750 g) beef short ribs
4 spring onions, shredded on the diagonal
5 garlic cloves, peeled, crushed, and finely chopped
1 in (2.5 cm) piece of fresh ginger, peeled, crushed, and finely chopped
2 tablespoons soy sauce
1 tablespoon sesame oil
1 tablespoon toasted sesame seeds
Freshly ground black pepper

---

1 tablespoon vegetable oil
Water

---

1 egg, beaten, fried, and cut into thin strips
2 spring onions, shredded on the diagonal

Chop or saw the short ribs into 2 in (5 cm) pieces if not already done so by your butcher. Score them deeply to the bone in diagonal slashes. Mix the spring onions, garlic, ginger, soy sauce, sesame oil, sesame seeds, and plenty of black pepper, and pour over the ribs. Coat well and leave aside to marinade for 2 hours or longer.

Heat the vegetable oil in a large pot and add the ribs. Fry to brown, turning frequently with tongs. Add the remaining marinade liquid and enough cold water to cover (about $1\frac{1}{2}$–2 pints/900 ml–1.2 litres). Bring to the boil and simmer for $1\frac{1}{2}$ hours or until the meat is tender. Spoon off the surface fat (or allow to cool and remove when hard).

Before serving, adjust seasoning, bring to the boil to reheat. Serve in individual bowls garnished with egg strips and shredded spring onions.

'Hangover Soup Alley'

After sessions drinking *bbaegal* (a particularly lethal Chinese spirit made from sorghum distilled to 150 proof) there was many an afternoon when Uncle Donald awoke with a mighty hangover to end all hangovers. However, fortunately in this traditional society there were cures at hand.

For example — one place and one place only in all of Seoul, apparently, specialized in *tung gol*, ox spinal cord, blanched lightly then dressed in soy sauce, sesame oil, and spring onions. 'Very rich in vitamin B,' says Donald fondly in recollection. *Tung gol* may well have been a great delicacy; more often than not, though, he and his drinking pals would head out to Chongjin-dong, an area behind the American Embassy where there was a small lane known as 'Hangover Soup Alley'. There, dozens of shops inevitably stayed open well after the hour of curfew (for this was during the period when all citizens were ordered to be off the streets after midnight). But there, in poky, dark little shacks, the men could lustily down bowls of *haejangguk* — 'hangover soup' made with fresh poached ox blood, a potent pick-me-up, before venturing out into the streets once more to dodge the imagined bullets of Korea under martial law.

KOMGUK BEEF AND TURNIP SOUP

곰 국

Another good, hearty but exceedingly simple winter soup.

1½ lb (750 g) beef brisket
1 large Korean or Chinese turnip, peeled
Water
4 spring onions, chopped
3 garlic cloves, peeled, crushed, and finely chopped
3 tablespoons soy sauce
1 tablespoon toasted sesame seeds
1 tablespoon sesame oil
Salt
Freshly ground black pepper

Put the brisket and the whole turnip into a large pot with about 3 pints (1½ litres) of water. Bring to the boil and simmer gently for 2 hours or until the meat is tender. Remove the meat and turnip from the pot, allow to cool, and cut into thin slices. Mix together the spring onions, garlic, soy sauce, sesame seeds, and sesame oil. Mix this well with the sliced meat and turnip. When the soup has cooled, skim off the fat and return the meat and vegetables to the pot. Bring to the boil once more and adjust the seasoning. Serve with steamed white rice.

WANJAGUK MEAT BALL SOUP

완자국

½ lb (250 g) lean minced beef
½ cake bean curd
3 garlic cloves, peeled, crushed, and finely chopped
2 teaspoons soy sauce
1 teaspoon sesame oil
2 spring onions, finely chopped
1 tablespoon toasted sesame seeds
Salt
1 egg, beaten
Flour

2½ pints (1.5 litres) homemade beef broth
Bunch of chives, snipped

Put the ground beef in a bowl. Wrap the bean curd in a clean piece of muslin and squeeze out excess water. Crumble this into the meat, together with the garlic, soy sauce, sesame oil, spring onions, sesame seeds, and salt to taste. Shape into 1 in (2.5 cm) meatballs. Dip each meatball into beaten egg, then into flour. Bring the beef broth to the boil, and spoon the meatballs in one at a time. Cook for about 10−15 minutes, or until cooked through. Serve in bowls, decorated with snipped chives.

OINAENGGUK CHILLED CUCUMBER SOUP

오 이 냉국

This simple, rather sharp cucumber soup is not unlike a Korean *gazpacho*, a most refreshing beverage on sultry summer days.

1 cucumber
Water
3 tablespoons rice or cider vinegar
2 teaspoons soy sauce
1 teaspoon sesame oil
2 teaspoons sugar
Salt
1 small red or green pepper, seeded, and finely chopped
2 spring onions, shredded on the diagonal
2 red chillies, seeded, and cut into thin strips
Ice cubes

Cut the cucumber into thin matchsticks. Pour about a pint of cold water into a bowl. Add the vinegar, soy sauce, sesame oil, sugar, and salt to taste. Mix well. Add the cucumber and chopped red or green pepper, then garnish with the spring onions and chillies. Chill well and add a few ice cubes to each bowl before serving.

The *Chokbo*, a Unique Family Genealogy
Korea is almost unique in the world in that most families keep written genealogies which trace its history through the male line back to their roots, in many cases hundreds of years ago. The details are meticulously recorded in the *chokbo*, a book — sometimes running to several volumes — which notes all births, marriages, offspring, and relevant occupational details such as levels of civil examinations passed. These details are usually recorded in Chinese, for centuries the language of scholars and the court.

Traditionally, the *chokbo* is passed down to and held by the eldest son in the family, a position that my cousin Bong Tae, eldest son of Halmoni's only brother, now occupies. Though there are admittedly millions of Kims in Korea, each belongs to a different clan. But it is only our line, the Kyongju Kims, who can claim to be direct 'royal descendants' of the kings of Silla, who unified the Korean peninsula in the eighth century. Nonetheless, I still can't help but feel just a little like Thomas Hardy's poor old Jack Durbey-field, late of the d'Urbervilles...

SHIGUMCHIGUK SPINACH SOUP

시금치국

$\frac{1}{4}$ lb (125 g) steak
2 tablespoons soy sauce
3 spring onions, finely chopped
2 garlic cloves, peeled, crushed, and finely chopped
1 teaspoon toasted sesame seeds
Freshly ground black pepper
1 tablespoon sesame oil
$\frac{3}{4}$ lb (375 g) fresh spinach, washed and trimmed
1 cake bean curd, diced into cubes
Salt
Water

Thinly slice the steak and mix together with the soy sauce, spring onions, garlic, sesame seeds, and black pepper. Leave to marinade for about 30 minutes. Heat the sesame oil in a large pot and fry the beef briefly until brown. Add about $2\frac{1}{2}$ pints ($1\frac{1}{4}$ litres) of water, bring to the boil, and cook until the meat is tender. Meanwhile, chop the spinach coarsely, and add to the soup, together with the diced bean curd, 5 minutes before serving. Simmer briefly until cooked through, season with salt to taste, and serve at once.

YACHAEGUK VEGETABLE SOUP

야채국

Simple *yachaeguk*, made with whatever fresh vegetables are at hand, is a delicious accompaniment to any home-style Korean meal.

$\frac{1}{4}$ lb (125 g) steak
2 tablespoons soy sauce
3 spring onions, shredded on the diagonal
2 garlic cloves, peeled, crushed, and finely chopped
1 teaspoon toasted sesame seeds
Freshly ground black pepper
1 tablespoon sesame oil
Water
3 carrots, peeled and roughly diced
1 onion, peeled and sliced

2 potatoes, peeled and roughly diced
4 courgettes, roughly diced
$\frac{1}{4}$ head Chinese cabbage, roughly cut into 1 in (2.5 cm) squares
Salt
Freshly ground black pepper

Thinly slice the steak. Mix together the soy sauce, shredded spring onions, garlic, sesame seeds, and black pepper. Pour this marinade over the meat and leave for 30 minutes. Heat the sesame oil in a large pot and briefly fry the steak until brown. Add about $2\frac{1}{2}$–3 pints ($1\frac{1}{4}$–$1\frac{1}{2}$ litres) of water and the prepared vegetables. Bring to the boil, and simmer until tender, about 30–40 minutes. Season with salt, if necessary, and freshly ground black pepper.

MAEUNTANG HOT FISH SOUP

매운 탕

In coastal villages all around Korea, whenever you order *saengsonhoe* – raw fish – you usually choose your specimen live from a tank. Then, after you have devoured it, the carcase is whisked away from the table and turned into a quick *maeuntang* – hot fish soup. The best *maeuntang*, however, we feel is one that is made to order, with a whole red snapper or sea bass, so that there are great tasty chunks of fish meat along with the fish- and chilli-flavoured broth. Then it is a virtual meal in itself.

1 whole red snapper or sea bass (about 1–$1\frac{1}{2}$ lb/500–750 g), cleaned
and scaled
$\frac{1}{4}$ lb (125 g) frying steak
$1\frac{1}{2}$ tablespoons *kochujang*
2 teaspoons sesame oil
1 tablespoon soy sauce
2 garlic cloves, peeled, crushed, and finely chopped
Freshly ground black pepper
1 tablespoon vegetable oil
Water
1 courgette, sliced on the diagonal
1 red pepper, seeded, and roughly diced
1 green pepper, seeded, and roughly diced
3–4 fresh chillies, seeded, and sliced
1 cake bean curd, diced
Salt
2 spring onions, shredded on the diagonal

Cut the fish into about 4−6 large pieces across the body. Thinly slice the steak. Mix the *kochujang*, sesame oil, soy sauce, garlic, and black pepper together with the sliced steak; leave for 30 minutes. Heat the vegetable oil in a large pot and fry the marinaded steak until brown, about 5 minutes. Add about $2\frac{1}{2}$ pints ($1\frac{1}{4}$ litres) water and bring to the boil. Add the fish, courgette, red and green peppers, and fresh chillies. Allow to simmer for 20−25 minutes, or until the fish is tender and cooked. Add the bean curd 5 minutes before serving. Adjust the seasoning and garnish with shredded spring onions.

MANDUGUK MEAT DUMPLINGS IN BROTH

만두국

Whenever we visit Halmoni, she always tries to have a steaming pot full of *mandu* for she knows it is a favourite of all of ours. *Mandu* are delicious served in rich chicken broth (*manduguk*); or else as left-overs, they can be lightly fried, and eaten with vinegar dipping sauce. When Koreans make *mandu* it is an event, with many hands sitting around the table together, making the filling, rolling out the paste, filling and folding the wrappers. Though purists may claim that the best *mandu* must be made with homemade wrappers, Halmoni says that *won ton* skins (available from oriental grocers) work just fine. This recipe may seem rather a lot, but *mandu* is something that you always make in large batches. Get an assembly line of family members going.

About 80 *won ton* skins

Filling
1 lb (500 g) lean ground pork
$\frac{1}{2}$ lb (250 g) lean ground beef
3 garlic cloves, peeled, crushed, and finely chopped
2 tablespoons soy sauce
4 tablespoons sesame oil
1 tablespoon toasted sesame seeds

1 in (2.5 cm) piece of fresh ginger, peeled, crushed, and finely chopped
10 spring onions, finely chopped
$\frac{1}{2}$ lb (250 g) *kimchi*, rinsed, finely chopped, then squeezed to remove excess moisture
$\frac{1}{4}$ lb (125 g) fresh bean sprouts, parboiled briefly, then finely chopped, and squeezed to remove excess moisture
1 cake bean curd, placed in a cheesecloth or muslin cloth and squeezed to drain out excess moisture
1 teaspoon salt
Plenty of freshly ground black pepper to taste

Chicken broth
1 chicken, rinsed and cleaned
2 tablespoons soy sauce
1 tablespoon sesame oil
1 teaspoon salt
Bunch of spring onions, cut into 3 in (7.5 cm) pieces
2 in (5 cm) piece of fresh ginger, peeled and sliced
4 pints (2 litres) water
4 spring onions, finely chopped

Gently fry the ground pork for five minutes to render the fat, then drain. Add this meat to a large bowl, together with the ground beef. Then add all the other ingredients for the filling and mix thoroughly with the hands.

Arrange a saucer of water in front of each person who is helping to fill the skins. To fill, take a *won ton* skin and dip the edges in the saucer of water to wet; take a heaped teaspoon of filling and place in the centre of each skin. Fold over and crimp the edges to seal. Continue until all the filling is used up.

Meanwhile, make the chicken broth: place the chicken in a large pot, together with the other ingredients, add water and bring to the boil. Skim, then simmer for $1\frac{1}{2}$–2 hours. Remove the chicken, and reserve the meat for another meal.

The *mandu* should be boiled separately from the soup in another large pot of water. Add some vegetable oil to the boiling water to keep from sticking, then add the *mandu* about 5 or 6 at a time, depending on the size of the pot. When the dumplings rise to the surface, they are done. Remove with a slotted spoon and set aside.

Place about 5 or 6 dumplings in each bowl, and ladle over the hot chicken broth. Garnish with chopped spring onions, and serve with *chojang* vinegar dipping sauce on the side. Or else serve the *mandu* separately, to be eaten dry with *chojang*. Left-over or cooked *mandu* can be frozen; de-frost and pan-fry, then serve with *chojang*.

CHATCHUK PINE NUT 'PORRIDGE'

잣 죽

This simple, rather bland pine nut 'porridge' might be served as part of a special Korean banquet, to be eaten alongside all the other dishes and *panchan*. Or else, make it to eat with a simple family supper, accompanied, perhaps, by some savoury grilled meat or vegetable fritters, *namul*, and *kimchi*.

1 cup rice
1 cup pine nuts
5 cups water
1 tablespoon sesame oil
1 teaspoon salt
Pine nuts to garnish

Place the rice in a pot and wash vigorously under running water for several minutes until all the excess starch has been washed out and the water runs clear. Cover with water and leave to soak for 2–3 hours, then drain.

Add 1 cup of water to the pine nuts and then grind them in a blender or food processor to a smooth paste. Add 2 cups of water to the rice, and grind in a blender to a smooth paste.

In a heavy-based pot, add the pine nut and rice mixtures, plus the sesame oil and remaining water (2 cups). Cook slowly over a low heat for about 45 minutes, stirring frequently. Season with salt to taste and garnish each bowl with a few pine nuts before serving hot.

CHONBOKCHUK ABALONE 'PORRIDGE'

전복죽

Abalone porridge, bland and chewy, makes a nutritious Korean breakfast, though indeed this and other such 'porridges' may be served at any meal.

2 cups rice
$\frac{1}{4}$ lb (125 g) tinned abalone
2 tablespoons sesame oil
1 teaspoon salt
7 cups water

Place the rice in a pot and wash vigorously under running water for several minutes until all the excess starch has been washed out and the water runs clear. Cover with water and leave to soak for 2−3 hours, then drain.

Finely dice the abalone. In a large pot, heat the sesame oil and sauté the abalone for 5 minutes. Add the soaked rice and salt and continue to sauté until well mixed and coated with oil. Add about half the water and cook very gently over a low heat. After half an hour, add the rest of the water and continue to simmer for a further 30 minutes, stirring from time to time. Serve hot with *chojang* vinegar soy sauce.

TWOENJANG-TCHIGAE SOY BEAN PASTE SOUP

된장찌게

In Seoul, the smell of homemade *twoenjang* — fermented soy bean paste — permeates the city. To the newcomer, it is a somewhat overpowering aroma to say the least, and definitely an acquired taste. Yet not to appreciate *twoenjang* as an essential flavouring ingredient and staple of the Korean kitchen is to miss the very soul of its cuisine. *Twoenjang-tchigae* is such common everyday fare that it is as essential — almost — as rice and *kimchi*. *Twoenjang* is available from Korean groceries already prepared, for those of us who don't happen to have our own *jang* terrace.

$\frac{1}{4}$ lb (125 g) steak
$\frac{1}{4}$ lb (125 g) *kimchi*
2 garlic cloves, peeled, crushed, and finely chopped
2 tablespoons soy sauce
1 tablespoon vegetable oil
2 tablespoons *twoenjang* (soy bean paste)
Water
1 cake bean curd, diced
2–4 green chillies, seeded and finely chopped
1 courgette, roughly diced
3 spring onions, shredded on the diagonal
Salt
Freshly ground black pepper

Thinly slice the steak. Cut the *kimchi* into similar-sized strips. Mix both together with the garlic and soy sauce. Heat the vegetable oil in a pot and gently fry the beef and *kimchi* for about 5 minutes or so. Add the *twoenjang*, stir to mix well, then pour on $1\frac{1}{2}$ pints (900 ml) of water and bring to the boil. Allow the soup to simmer for 15–20 minutes. About 5 minutes before serving, add the bean curd, chillies, courgette, and spring onions (reserving some for a garnish). Season with salt and pepper to taste. Serve in bowls garnished with a little spring onion.

Drinking tent at Haeundae Beach, near Pusan

Making *pajon* — spring onion pancake — on an outdoor griddle

Kalbi — marinated barbecued short ribs — together
with traditional accompaniments, *namul* and *kimchi*

The *jang* terrace

Chapchae a delicious noodle and vegetable medley

Namedaemun Sijang:
Great South Gate Market

Plaited bundles of sweet potato stems
to be made into *namul* or *kimchi*

Dried fish, still an everyday staple of
the Korean diet

Korean cabbage, turnips, and spring onions, the essential ingredients for winter *kimchi*

Wild edible mountain foods: bundles of *kosari* (fern bracken) and mushrooms

Red peppers hung from a doorway, a traditional symbol that a boy child has been born

Ploughing the rice paddies

Fresh ginseng rootlets

Squid hung out to dry at the East Coast fishing village of Sokcho

The Hyangwon pavilion at Kyongbok Palace, one of three remaining royal palaces in Seoul

TUBU-TCHIGAE BEAN CURD STEW

두부찌개

Tubu-tchigae is a classic, the sort of everyday food that Koreans yearn for when they have been away from home too long. When Halmoni prepared this for Syngman Rhee, the then first President of the Republic of Korea, he sighed in ecstasy and nostalgia (the man, a slight, skinny figure from pictures I have seen, had an immense and almost insatiable appetite, remembers Halmoni). Halmoni's *tubu-tchigae* is exceedingly simple to prepare, but its taste is authentic and truly delicious.

$1-1\frac{1}{2}$ cakes firm bean curd

$2-3$ loin pork chops, on the bone (about 1 lb/500 g)
Salt
Freshly ground black pepper
1 tablespoon vegetable oil
2 heaped tablespoons *kochujang*
3 cloves garlic, peeled, crushed, and finely chopped
1 in (2.5 cm) piece of fresh ginger, peeled, crushed, and finely chopped
1 tablespoon soy sauce
1 tablespoon sesame oil
About $\frac{1}{2}$ pint (300 ml) meat broth

---

2 stalks celery, sliced on the diagonal
1 green pepper, seeded and sliced on the diagonal
1 courgette, sliced on the diagonal
$2-3$ fresh chillies, seeded and sliced
3 spring onions, shredded on the diagonal

Cut the bean curd into cubes and set aside. Trim the pork chops of all fat, and cut into thick matchsticks. Use the trimmings and the bones to make a meat broth, if no other homemade broth is available; season with salt and plenty of freshly ground black pepper.

Heat the vegetable oil in a pot and fry the meat for 5 minutes or until brown. Add the *kochujang*, garlic, ginger, soy sauce, and sesame oil and cook over a medium flame for about 10 minutes, stirring all the while. Add meat broth, bring to the boil, then reduce to a simmer and add the celery, green pepper, courgette, and chillies. Simmer for about $25-30$ minutes. Add the bean curd to the pot 5 minutes before ready to serve. Simmer, then transfer to a large bowl. Garnish with shredded spring onions.

CHONGOL KOREAN MEAT AND VEGETABLE HOT POT

전골

Chongol, Korea's version of *sukiyaki*, is a one-pot meal, traditionally prepared over a burner at the table. Any number of ingredients can be added to the simmering deep and wide pan of cooking broth: this is Halmoni's version, a most substantial and festive feast which includes strips of meat, a variety of vegetables, bean curd, and *konnyaku*. As such, it is an ever popular and rather theatrical party favourite. But *chongol* is the sort of dish where you can utilize whatever is at hand, to make it as grand or as simple as you like.

Cooking broth
¼ pint (150 ml) rice wine or dry cooking sherry
¼ pint (150 ml) soy sauce
½ pint (300 ml) beef broth or chicken broth or water
2 heaped tablespoons sugar

---

1 lb (500 g) sirloin steak, cut against the grain into thin strips
3 stalks celery, cut into diagonal strips
2 carrots, peeled and cut into diagonal slices
1 large tin bamboo shoot (in one piece), sliced into large matchsticks
(squeeze out any excess moisture)
2 small white onions, peeled, halved, and cut into thin slices
½ lb (250 g) fresh *shiitake* mushrooms, sliced (if not available
substitute 10–15 dried Chinese mushrooms, cleaned, trimmed, and
soaked for 1–2 hours or until soft, then sliced)
About 15 spring onions, cut into 2 in (5 cm) long pieces
½ Chinese cabbage, cut into 1 in (2.5 cm) wide pieces
1 lb (500 g) spinach
2 cakes bean curd, cut in half horizontally, then sliced
1 cake *konnyaku* cut into thin slices

Chongol should be prepared in a large flat pan set over a burner at the table, if possible. Otherwise, cook then transfer to a bowl and serve immediately. It will be necessary to cook this amount in 2 or 3 batches, so divide the ingredients accordingly.

First prepare the cooking broth by adding the ingredients to a pot and simmering for 10 minutes.

In a large pan or pot, heat 1 tablespoon oil, and stir-fry the sliced steak for a few minutes to brown. Next add the hard vegetables to the pan, celery, carrots, bamboo shoots, sliced onions, and dried mushrooms (if not using fresh). Add a few ladles of the cooking broth, bring to the boil and simmer for about 5 minutes.

Next add the fresh mushrooms, spring onions, cabbage and spinach and cook for a further 2−3 minutes, adding more cooking broth as necessary. Finally add the *konnyaku* and bean curd and cook for a further 2−3 minutes. Stir well to coat with sauce and serve immediately.

Continue cooking in batches until all the ingredients are finished.

Journal Notes

The Lotte Department Store

The Lotte Department Store, located in the heart of downtown Myong-dong, is a most remarkable emporium. Ten floors, plus two basements, are stocked with just about anything you might care to buy — from traditional Korean handicrafts, to sporting goods, householdware, and high fashion clothing. The food hall in the basement is a labyrinth where you can find everything from a range of ready-prepared kimchis *and lines of strung-up dried fish, to Western convenience foods, cheeses, and — to our great delight — cornflakes.*

Tonight we were in the Lotte at closing hour, a most unusual experience. While the national anthem played over a loudspeaker, all the staff, smart in their blue uniforms and white gloves, stood stiffly to attention. Then, as we walked from the store, they one by one bowed low and deep to us. We nodded to each and waved as we passed, feeling, I have to admit, a little embarrassed, but also rather regal, on our brief unscheduled walkabout. 'Now I know what the Queen feels like,' said Kim.

TUBUJONGOL BEAN CURD HOT-POT

두부전골

This is a special and delicious dish; for the packets of bean curd, stuffed with seasoned meat and tied up with spring onion ribbons, then cooked in broth at the table with other vegetables, are both attractive and really tasty.

2 cakes firm bean curd
1 tablespoon flour
1 tablespoon vegetable oil

$\frac{1}{4}$ lb (125 g) lean minced beef
2 tablespoons soy sauce
1 tablespoon sesame oil
1 teaspoon toasted sesame seeds
1 garlic clove, peeled, crushed, and finely chopped
2 spring onions, finely chopped
Freshly ground black pepper

---

10 large spring onions

---

2 carrots, peeled and sliced on the diagonal
2 courgettes, sliced on the diagonal
2 red chillies, seeded and cut into strips
1 onion, peeled, halved, and sliced lengthwise
$\frac{1}{4}$ lb (125 g) fresh mushrooms, sliced
$1\frac{1}{2}$ pints (900 ml) boiling homemade beef broth
Salt
Freshly ground black pepper
2 eggs, beaten, fried, and sliced into strips
3 spring onions, sliced on the diagonal

Slice each cake of bean curd horizontally into slices $\frac{1}{4}$ in (6 mm) thick, about 5 slices per cake. Dredge each slice lightly in flour, then fry in hot oil for 2−3 minutes a side or until brown. Drain and set aside.

Mix the ground beef with the seasonings and leave to marinade for 30 minutes, then stir-fry for about 5−7 minutes or until cooked. Drain off excess fat.

Cut off the stalks of the spring onions, and plunge them into boiling water to blanch for 1 minute.

Make bean curd 'sandwiches' by placing a tablespoon or so of the meat filling on one slice of bean curd, covering it with another slice, and tying the parcels up with blanched spring onion stalks.

Arrange these bean curd bundles, together with the sliced

carrots, courgettes, chillies, onion, and mushrooms, attractively in a casserole or wok (if you have a table-top burner, then this dish can be prepared at the table). Pour on the boiling stock and cook over a high heat for 10 minutes. Season to taste, garnish with egg strips and spring onions, and serve hot from the casserole.

5
Kimchi and *Namul*

It is autumn once more, time again for the annual preservation of winter vegetables, the *kimjang*, or *kimchi*-making period. Halmoni remembers clearly what an important and busy time this always was. Indeed, it would take the better part of a week to prepare the *kimchi* for one winter. First, she, and those sisters who were still at home, accompanied First Mother and Little Mother down from the mountain house to the market at Sochang. There the streets were piled high with mountains of great Korean cabbage, mounds of giant white radishes, piles of pungent spring onions and knobbly fresh ginger root, and braided ropes of garlic. First Mother prodded the vegetables with the stem of her pipe, checking and rejecting this lot of onions, accepting those cabbages, haggling fiercely over the price, then − bargain struck, pipe lit, hands folded − she instructed them to be loaded onto the *chige* − the wooden A-frame − that was strapped to the back of the old male servant who had accompanied them down from the mountain. By the time she was finished, that *chige* would be piled high, the poor old man bent double under the considerable load. But this was to be expected, for after all, it was the *kimjang* − the time to make enough winter *kimchi* to last through to spring.

Back home, the labour began: first seeding the dried chillies by hand, then pounding, pounding, pounding them into a coarse red pepper powder. The women all wore handkerchiefs over their faces, for the red dust was potent and painful to inhale. If you got some pepper dust on your hands, then scratched your eyes, it would burn for days. The knobbly ginger roots had to be peeled, the fat, juicy cloves of garlic, too, then both were pounded to a pungent pulp with a pestle in a great wooden mortar.

Piles and piles of spring onions had to be stripped, then shredded on the diagonal, the giant white radishes, peeled and grated by hand. And, of course, the piles of cabbages were all split and quartered, then interleaved with coarse sea salt and left to wilt. First Mother inspected the whole operation, bending a bit of cabbage in her hands to see if it was yet ready, scolding a sister for not shredding the *muu* finely enough, or rapping Little Mother on the head with the bowl of her long brass pipe. She was, Halmoni remembers, always rapping poor Little Mother with her pipe and scolding her, whether or not she deserved it.

The *kimchi* seasonings — red pepper powder, garlic, ginger and soused fermented anchovies — were all mixed in enormous tubs by hand. Once the cabbage had sufficiently wilted and been rinsed, the women sat together, painstakingly interleaving this pungent stuffing in between the leaves of the wilted cabbage.

When they had all been so prepared, the cabbages were packed tightly into large earthenware jars, jars so large, remembers Halmoni, that they were even taller than she. These jars were then covered with more wilted cabbage leaves, a weight was placed on top, then they were buried into pits dug into the ground. This allowed the cabbage mixture to ferment at just the right, slow pace, and also kept the *kimchi* from freezing during winters that were often bitterly cold.

'This winter *kimchi*,' Halmoni says, 'would last through to March, but by that time it was very sour. We were always happy when spring came and we could make *tongchimi* — refreshing, clean white radish water *kimchi*, made with no chillies or garlic.'

Kimchi, of course, is the most famous manifestation of Korean food, and, indeed, Korean methods of preserving vegetables, fish, and shellfish through salting and natural fermentation are distinctive and unique. Virtually anything at all can be and is *kimchied* including watermelon, sole, crab, chicken, or pheasant, as well as the more usual vegetables — cabbage, radish, spinach, cucumber, watercress, or leeks.

Namuls, fresh salads, or lightly steamed or fried vegetables, are an equally important feature of Korean food. If *kimchi* must, on the whole, be made some days (or in some cases a week or weeks) in advance, a selection of tasty, savoury *namul* can always be prepared from whatever fresh vegetables are at hand. Dried vegetables, herbs and roots are also used extensively to make *namuls*. Do try and purchase such unusual but typical and delicious Korean specialities such as *kosari* and *toraji*. Or do as the Koreans, and gather them yourself in the wilds.

HALMONI'S QUICK AND EASY *KIMCHI*

김치와 나물

To make real, old-style winter *kimchi*, says Halmoni, is a difficult and time-consuming task. Indeed, the *kimjangs* which she remembers were annual events that lasted for many days, and called for many hands to interleave painstakingly the salted cabbage leaves with mixtures of ginger, garlic, red pepper powder, and soused fish. Not only that, the quantities made were immense, packed into great earthenware Ali Baba-style jars, enough to last right through from autumn to early spring. These days, though, Halmoni has devised this quick and easy but authentic *kimchi* which is virtually foolproof and always delicious.

1 large Chinese cabbage (about $3\frac{1}{2}$–4 lb/$1\frac{3}{4}$–2 kg)
3 tablespoons salt
2 tablespoons coarse red pepper powder
About 6 oz (175 g) preserved soused anchovies (available from Korean groceries, or else substitute 3 tablespoons anchovy essence)
5 garlic cloves, peeled, crushed, and finely chopped
2 in (5 cm) piece of fresh ginger, peeled, crushed, and finely chopped
2 teaspoons sugar

Trim off the tough outer leaves and stem of the Chinese cabbage. Cut lengthwise into quarters, then slice into 2 in (5 cm) pieces. Place in a large bowl and sprinkle with the salt. Mix well with the hands. Leave the cabbage for some hours, shaking the bowl from time to time and mixing well with the hands. Drain off any excess water that collects. Keep checking the cabbage, bending the thicker parts of the leaves to see if they have yet sufficiently wilted: they should be limp, yet should still be crisp when broken. The usual time, says Halmoni, is around 4 hours.

Meanwhile, take the red pepper powder, place in a saucer, and add sufficient water to make a paste. It is important to do this well before you want to use it, to draw out the colour — if you remember, do this overnight.

If using the soused fermented anchovies, place in a pan and bring to the boil. Simmer for about 15 minutes, then strain the juice through muslin or cheesecloth, pressing out all the juice and flavour from the fish. Save the juice and discard the remains of the fish. If using bottled anchovy essence then this step is not necessary; simply use the essence in place of the strained juice.

When the cabbage is ready, rinse well and drain in a colander for about 30 minutes. Keep aside a few nice large cabbage leaves to seal the mixture with. Next, mix together the fish juice or anchovy essence, garlic, ginger, sugar, and red pepper powder paste. Add this mixture to the drained cabbage and mix well (if using your hands, it is advisable to wear rubber gloves!). Pack tightly into sterile jars, seal with the cabbage leaves that had been laid aside, and cover with cellophane and lids.

Place the jars in a cool, dark, dry spot. The time that the *kimchi* will require is a matter of both fine judgment, personal taste, and prevailing weather conditions. In warm weather, says Halmoni, a period of hours, perhaps, or just a day might be sufficient to ferment the mixture. In winter, on the other hand, a period of 5—7 days might be required (though much less in centrally heated houses). In mild spring or autumn weather, a period of 2—3 days is usually about right. Moreover, some like their *kimchi* really sour, others prefer a fresher, crunchier version. Experiment until you achieve the desired results. Once the cabbage has fermented, wrap the tightly covered jars in plastic bags sealed with rubber bands (to keep the pervasive smell from invading the whole house), and place in the refrigerator.

The amount of time that *kimchi* will last is also a question of taste. Some people like really ripe *kimchi*; we, on the other hand, prefer fresher, crunchier versions. Though purists claim that *kimchi* will last indefinitely, nonetheless, we advise never to keep *kimchi* any longer than you feel comfortable with (this may be only a matter of days, or a week, or longer). But we certainly advise never eating *kimchi* that is too sour. To serve, place *kimchi* in small saucers as an accompaniment to meals.

KKAKTTUGI CUBED RADISH KIMCHI

깍두기

After cabbage *kimchi*, *kkakttugi* seems to me to be the next most frequently encountered variety. It is a delicious, easy-to-eat dish of cubed and salted radish chunks seasoned with red pepper powder, soused anchovies, garlic, and ginger. *Kkakttugi* is easy to make, too.

**1 large Korean radish, peeled
2 tablespoons salt
2 tablespoons red pepper powder
2 tablespoons soused anchovy juice (see previous recipe) or 1 tablespoon anchovy essence
2 garlic cloves, peeled, crushed, and finely chopped
1 in (2.5 cm) piece of fresh ginger, peeled, crushed, and finely chopped
4 spring onions, cut into 2 in (5 cm) pieces**

Cut the peeled Korean radish into $\frac{1}{2}$–1 in (1.2 cm–2.5 cm) cubes. Place in a bowl and sprinkle with salt. Set aside for about 2 hours.

Soak the red pepper powder in water to draw out the colour. Mix together with the anchovy juice or essence, garlic, and ginger. Rinse the radish cubes well in fresh water, place in a clean bowl, and add the seasoning mixture, and the spring onion pieces. Mix well, then pack into sterile jars, seal with cellophane and lids, and place in a cool dry spot. As above, the time required will vary, though in mild weather about 2–3 days should suffice. When ready, place jars in plastic bags, seal, and put in the refrigerator.

OISOBAGI STUFFED CUCUMBER KIMCHI

오이소박이

Oisobagi – stuffed cucumber *kimchi* – is another all-time favourite of mine. The key to making really good cucumber *kimchi*, advises Halmoni, is to pour boiling water over the cucumbers after they have been salted. This, for some reason, keeps them really crisp and crunchy for a longer period.

6 cucumbers (about 8 in/20 cm long)
3 tablespoons salt
6 spring onions, chopped
3 garlic cloves, peeled, crushed, and finely chopped
1 in (2.5 cm) piece of fresh ginger, peeled, crushed, and finely chopped
1 small Korean radish, cut into fine matchsticks
4 tablespoons red pepper powder
1 tablespoon sugar

Cut the cucumbers either in half (if small), or in thirds (if large). Stand each segment on its end, and cut a cross down each one almost to the base (but do not separate). Sprinkle the cucumbers with the salt, and rub well in. Cover and set aside for about 2 hours (the time this takes depends on factors such as humidity and moisture-level in the cucumbers). They should be wilted, but still have a 'snap' when bent. When the cucumbers are sufficiently salted, wipe off the excess salt, then pour boiling water over them. Rinse well and refresh immediately in cold water.

Mix together the spring onions, garlic, ginger, radish, red pepper powder, and sugar. Wipe dry the cucumbers and stuff the mixture into the slits in each. Pack the stuffed cucumbers into sterile jars and cover tightly. Allow to stand in a cool, dark place for at least a day, then transfer to a refrigerator. Serve well chilled. These pickled cucumbers will last for at least a few days, but they are at their best before they go soft or mushy.

Regional Variations

Each region has its own particular variations of *kimchi*. In and around Seoul and Kyonggi-do, for example, *kimchi* includes ingredients such as abalone, gingko and pine nuts, and pickled raw fish. In the northwest of the peninsula (North Korea's Pyongyang region), on the other hand, the water is said to be exceptionally pure, and there spices and flavourings are used sparingly to result in refreshing *kimchi* which is clean and unsalty. *Tongchimi* — water radish *kimchi* — is the mild and outstanding speciality of this region. In the Cholla provinces to the southwest, on the other hand, where the climate is considerably hotter, *kimchi* is traditionally made with both more salt and more red pepper powder, essential to ensure adequate preservation. These features are also true of *kimchi* from Kyongsang-do, Halmoni's home region, where pickled and fermented fish is usually also added to the mix.

TONGCHIMI RADISH WATER KIMCHI

동 치 미

At the Nampo Myunok, a simple drinking and eating house located in the warren of alleys behind Seoul's City Hall, there is a line of about a dozen earthenware jars buried alongside the corridor as you enter. All are receptacles for *tongchimi*, a mild, crunchy radish water *kimchi*. Each jar bears the date of when each batch was made. This demonstrates how fickle and intuitive an art making *kimchi* is.

'How long does it take to make *tongchimi?*' I asked. 'About seven days in warm weather,' the proprietor told us. 'No, five in late spring,' his wife interjected. 'Ten in winter. Sometimes longer.' We sampled a variety from the jars and could indeed taste the difference: radish left in the brine mixture for too long is soft and not so fresh and crunchy. Not enough time and it has no flavour. But just right and it is superb: crisp, fresh, and sour at the same time.

10 small Korean radishes
12 oz (375 g) coarse sea salt
24 spring onions
4 in (10 cm) piece of fresh ginger, peeled and sliced
Water

Select young, tender Korean radishes. Remove any roots, scrape them, and wash. Roll the whole radishes in the coarse salt and leave overnight, turning them occasionally. The next day, rinse off the salt, mix with the spring onions, and ginger, place in a large sterile crock or glass jar, and cover with water. Place a plate over the top to ensure that the vegetables stay submerged. Leave in a cool, dark place for about 2−3 days in warm weather, or a week in winter. To serve, slice the radishes and serve a few slices plus a piece of spring onion in individual glass bowls, topped up with the *tongchimi* water. This simple food is usually eaten at the start of the meal to whet the appetite.

NABAK-KIMCHI FRESH WATER KIMCHI

나박김치

This simple water *kimchi* is exceedingly fresh, crispy, and delicious; indeed for many who consider *kimchi* to be a fearsome and acquired taste, it comes as something of a revelation. But to make really good *nabak-kimchi* it is essential that you choose the very freshest ingredients.

Half a small Chinese cabbage
1 medium Korean radish
1 tablespoon salt
3 spring onions, shredded on the diagonal
3 garlic cloves, peeled, crushed, and finely chopped
1 in (2.5 cm) piece of fresh ginger, peeled, crushed, and finely chopped
2 fresh red chillies, seeded and cut into very thin strips
1 tablespoon red pepper powder
$1\frac{1}{2}$ pints (900 ml) water
2 tablespoons salt
1 tablespoon sugar

Wash the cabbage and cut into 1 in (2.5 cm) squares. Peel and slice the radish into similar-sized pieces. Sprinkle with 1 tablespoon salt, mix well, and leave to stand for 30 minutes. Rinse well and drain.

In a large clean bowl, add the cabbage, radish, spring onions, garlic, ginger, chillies, and red pepper powder. Mix well. Add the water, salt, and sugar. Cover and leave to stand in cool, dark place for 1 or 2 days (depending on the weather — in very warm weather a few hours may be sufficient). Bottle in sterile jars and store in the refrigerator.

To serve, give each person a small bowl of their own water *kimchi*. Serve with the vegetables floating in the water which itself can be drunk from the bowl if desired. Like *tongchimi*, *nabak-kimchi* makes a refreshing and appetizing opening to a Korean meal.

FRESH INSTANT *KIMCHI*

나박김치

'Even *haoles* like this fresh instant *kimchi*!' says Halmoni. Perhaps that is because this invention of hers is really more like a dressed Western salad. Certainly this instant *kimchi* makes a more than adequate stand-in for those times when you happen to be out of fermented cabbage *kimchi*.

$\frac{1}{2}$ head Chinese cabbage
$\frac{1}{2}$ head Cos lettuce
6 spring onions, shredded on the diagonal

2 tablespoons rice or cider vinegar
3 tablespoons soy sauce
2 tablespoons sesame oil
$\frac{1}{2}$–1 tablespoon red pepper powder
2 teaspoons toasted sesame seeds

Break up the Chinese cabbage and the lettuce into strips. Place in a large bowl together with the shredded spring onions. Mix together the dressing ingredients, pour over, and toss well just before eating.

SHIGUMCHINAMUL SPINACH SALAD

시금치나물

Vegetables, lightly steamed or blanched, then dressed simply in soy sauce and sesame oil, form an important and delicious part of the Korean diet. Spinach lends itself particularly well to this treatment, but also try this same method with any other vegetables in season.

1 lb (500 g) young spinach, washed and trimmed of tough stems

2 tablespoons soy sauce
1 tablespoon sesame oil
1 teaspoon sugar
2 teaspoons toasted sesame seeds

Steam the spinach for only a few minutes until tender. Drain immediately, then squeeze dry with the hands. Slice roughly. Mix the dressing ingredients together and pour over the spinach. Mix well. Serve warm or chilled.

MINARINAMUL WATERCRESS SALAD

미나리나물

Minari — watercress — is another favourite Korean vegetable. Though in the West it is almost always enjoyed as a raw salad ingredient, we think it is delicious blanched and dressed in soy sauce and sesame oil.

2 bunches watercress (about $\frac{1}{2}$ lb/250 g)

2 tablespoons soy sauce
1 tablespoon sesame oil
1 teaspoon sugar
1 garlic clove, peeled, crushed, and finely chopped
2 teaspoons toasted sesame seeds

Steam the watercress for 1 or 2 minutes only. Drain and refresh under cold water. Squeeze dry and roughly chop. Mix together the dressing ingredients and pour over the watercress. Mix well and chill before serving.

OINAMUL CUCUMBER SALAD

오이나물

This method of salting cucumbers in brine to make them extra crisp is popular not just in Korea, but also in countries as diverse as Denmark and Hungary. Make this refreshing salad as hot as you like, and experiment by adding other vegetables such as mild sliced onions, spring onions, carrot slices, or fresh chillies.

1 large cucumber or 2 small cucumbers
2 tablespoons salt
2 tablespoons rice or cider vinegar
1 tablespoon sugar
1−2 teaspoons red pepper powder, or to taste

Peel the cucumber and slice it as thinly as possible (we use a mandoline for this task). Place the cucumber slices in a bowl, sprinkle with the salt, and add water to cover. Leave to soak for 20−30 minutes. Drain, rinse, then wring as much moisture out of the cucumbers as you can by squeezing hard with the hands. Return to a clean bowl, add the vinegar, sugar, and red pepper powder to taste. Mix well and chill before serving.

MUUSAENGCHAE I KOREAN RADISH SALAD

무 우 생채

Muusaengchae is a characteristic and popular salad which always makes a good side accompaniment to a Korean meal. Indeed, it is a good quick substitute for *kimchi*.

1 Korean radish, peeled
1 tablespoon salt

---

1 garlic clove, peeled, crushed, and finely chopped
$\frac{1}{2}$in (12 mm) piece of fresh ginger, peeled, crushed, and finely chopped
$\frac{1}{2}$ tablespoon *kochujang*
2 teaspoons sugar
1 tablespoon rice or cider vinegar
1 tablespoon soy sauce
2 teaspoons toasted sesame seeds

---

2 springs onions, shredded on the diagonal

Grate or slice the Korean radish into long, thin strips. Place in a large bowl, add the salt, and mix well. Leave for about 10 minutes, then rinse well and squeeze out all the moisture. Return to a clean bowl.

Mix the dressing ingredients together and add to the shredded radish. Mix well. Garnish with the shredded spring onion. Chill before serving.

MUUSAENGCHAE II KOREAN RADISH SALAD

무우 샛채

Another version of this always popular salad.

1 Korean radish, peeled
1 tablespoon salt

$\frac{1}{2}$**in (12 mm) piece of fresh root ginger, peeled, crushed, and finely**
chopped
1 teaspoon red pepper powder
1 tablespoon sugar
4 tablespoons rice or cider vinegar
1 tablespoon sesame oil

---

2 teaspoons toasted sesame seeds

Grate or slice the Korean radish into long, thin strips. Place in a large bowl, add the salt, and mix well. Leave for about 10 minutes, then rinse well and squeeze out all the moisture. Return to a clean bowl.

Mix the dressing ingredients together and add to the shredded radish. Mix well. Garnish with toasted sesame seeds. Chill before serving.

SUNMUNAMUL KOREAN TURNIP SALAD

순 무 우 나물

Another typical but exceedingly simple salad. *Sunmu* is the large, round Korean turnip, here cooked lightly in sesame oil and soy sauce. Unlike most *namul*, the texture of this salad is rather soft, not crisp.

1 large Korean turnip (about 1 lb/500 g)
2 tablespoons sesame oil
2 tablespoons soy sauce
2 teaspoons sugar
2 teaspoons toasted sesame seeds

Peel the turnip and grate or slice into long, thin strips. Squeeze out excess moisture. Heat the sesame oil in a pot and add the turnip. Mix well and fry lightly for about 5 minutes. Add the soy sauce, sugar, and toasted sesame seeds. Mix well and serve at room temperature.

KAJINAMUL STEAMED AUBERGINE SALAD

가지나물

Simple steamed strips of aubergine, dressed with soy sauce and sesame oil, make a delicious and quick Korean side dish.

1 medium aubergine (or 2 small ones)
2 tablespoons soy sauce
1 tablespoon sesame oil
1 spring onion, finely chopped
1 garlic clove, peeled, crushed, and finely chopped
1 teaspoon toasted sesame seeds
1 teaspoon rice or cider vinegar

Wash the aubergines then steam until tender, about 10 minutes. Allow to cool, then slice lengthwise, and tear the flesh into thin strips. Squeeze out excess moisture and place in a bowl. Mix together remaining ingredients and add to the aubergine strips. Mix well and chill before serving.

SAENGCHAE THREE VEGETABLE SALAD

새 채

Saengchae — fresh Korean 'coleslaw': simple and tasty.

2 large carrots, peeled
2 stalks celery, string if necessary
¼ lb (125 g) Chinese cabbage
1 teaspoon salt
2 teaspoons sugar
2 tablespoons cider vinegar

Cut the carrots and celery into 2 in (5 cm) lengths, then into thin matchsticks. Shred the cabbage finely to about the same size. Combine the salt, sugar, and vinegar, then pour over the prepared vegetables to dress. Serve chilled.

SSUKKATMUCHIM GARLAND CHRYSANTHEMUM SALAD

쑥갓무침

Ssukka is a characteristically Korean vegetable that may be available at Korean groceries and other oriental food shops. It has a distinctive flavour somewhat between spinach and seaweed. Young leaves can be eaten raw, as a *ssam* 'roll up' wrapper for *pulgogi*, rice, and *kochujang*. However, as a cooked salad, it is equally delicious. Do note, however: garland chrysanthemum is no relation to our domestic chrysanthemum flower, which is highly poisonous!

1 bunch of *ssukka*, washed and trimmed of any tough stems

2 tablespoons soy sauce
1 tablespoon sesame oil
2 teaspoons toasted sesame seeds

Bring a pot of water to the boil and plunge the *ssukka* into it. Cook briefly for 1 or 2 minutes. Remove, refresh under cold water, and squeeze out excess moisture. Slice roughly.

Mix the dressing ingredients together, and add to the cooked *ssukka*. Serve warm or cold.

How to Sprout Beans

Though fresh mung bean sprouts may be widely available, soy bean and other sprouts are less so; but they are all very easy to grow at home. Moreover, we find that sprouted lentils, alfalfa, aduki beans, chick peas, and other beans, all make delicious Korean-style *namul*, steamed lightly, then dressed simply with soy sauce, sesame oil, and toasted sesame seeds.

To sprout beans, simply place about two tablespoons in a large jar. Secure a piece of muslin or cheesecloth over the mouth of the jar with a rubber band. Fill the jar with tepid water, place in a dark spot (like a cupboard) and leave for about eight hours. Drain the water out through the muslin. Rinse the beans again with tepid water, drain, and return to the dark spot. Continue to rinse about four times a day. After three or four days, the sprouts should be ready to eat.

KONGNAMULMUCHIM SOY BEAN SPROUT SALAD

콩나물무침

Soy bean sprouts are considerably larger than mung bean sprouts, and have an altogether deeper, rounder flavour. They are used extensively in the Korean kitchen and form an important part of the daily diet.

$\frac{1}{2}$ lb (250 g) soy bean sprouts

---

1 tablespoon soy sauce
$\frac{1}{2}$ tablespoon sesame oil
$\frac{1}{2}$ teaspoon rice vinegar
$\frac{1}{2}$ teaspoon sugar
1 teaspoon toasted sesame seeds

Remove the little rootlets from the ends of the soy bean sprouts. Heat a pot of boiling water and plunge the sprouts into it for $2-3$ minutes, taking care not to overcook them. Drain and refresh under cold water. Squeeze out excess moisture. Mix the dressing ingredients together, add to the sprouts, and mix well.

SUKCHUNAMUL MUNG BEAN SPROUT SALAD

숙주나물

$\frac{1}{2}$ lb (250 g) mung bean sprouts

---

1 tablespoon soy sauce
$\frac{1}{2}$ tablespoon sesame oil
1 teaspoon toasted sesame seeds
1 garlic clove, peeled, crushed, and finely chopped
1 teaspoon red pepper threads

Remove the little rootlets from the ends of the mung bean sprouts. Heat a pot of boiling water and plunge the sprouts in it, then remove immediately and drain in a colander. Refresh with cold water, then squeeze out excess moisture. Mix the dressing ingredients, add to the sprouts, and mix well.

MIYOKNAMUL SEAWEED SALAD

미역나물

Koreans are great lovers of seaweed: indeed all around this slender peninsula, immense quantities are harvested to be eaten fresh, or to be dried and salted for use as *namul*, or to be added to soups or *tchigae*. Dried seaweed is widely available from Korean groceries.

$\frac{1}{2}$ packet Korean brown seaweed (*miyok*), about 2 oz (50 g)

---

2 tablespoons soy sauce
1 tablespoon sesame oil
1 tablespoon rice or cider vinegar
1 tablespoon toasted sesame seeds

Wash the *miyok* in several changes of running water, rubbing it vigorously with the hands all the while to remove the salt. Slice it into fine pieces and wash again, then drain thoroughly, squeezing out excess moisture.

Mix the dressing ingredients and add to the *miyok*. Mix well and chill before serving.

An Unfortunate Incident

It is a well-known fact that Koreans — wherever they are — enjoy nothing more than to go hiking in the woods in search of wild edible greens, herbs, and roots. We have friends in central London who spend their weekends rootling around Richmond Park in search of *kosari* — edible fern bracken. In Korea itself, the sport of searching for edible wild mushrooms and other such foods is virtually a national pastime. And of course, Halmoni and her friends used to love to go out and gather such foods, too, in Hawaii and later in Los Angeles.

However, Halmoni has a sad story to tell of one such adventure. Once she and three others, including Sei Sook, an old friend from Honolulu days, went for the day to Big Bear Lake in the mountains outside Los Angeles. It was a mild day in spring, and the conditions and season were prefect for gathering royal fern bracken, known also as fiddleheads. Once there, they decided to split up in order to cover the ground more efficiently. Towards dusk, baskets full of the delicious fiddleheads, they all reassembled at the appointed spot — except for Sei Sook. She never turned up. To this day, no one knows what happened to her.

I asked Halmoni if she ate the fiddleheads gathered at such cost. 'Yes,' she admitted, though perhaps a trifle sheepishly. I feel certain that her friend Sei Sook would have understood.

KOSARINAMUL FERN BRACKEN SALAD

고사리나물

Edible fern bracken is but one of the many wild foods which Koreans are particularly fond of. High on mountain paths, at Sorak-san, Kaya-san and elsewhere, enterprising women who have been up early to gather these ferns, sell bundles of *kosari*, *toraji*, and much else, all to be eaten fresh or reconstituted at home and made into delicious *namul*. *Kosari* is available dried from Korean groceries. However, royal fern bracken — what we know as fiddleheads — is sometimes available fresh from speciality stores; if available, parboil it, then dress in soy sauce and sesame oil for a very special treat.

$\frac{1}{2}$ packet dried *kosari* (about 2 oz/50 g)
2 tablespoons sesame oil
1 tablespoon soy sauce

2 tablespoons chicken broth or water
2 teaspoons toasted sesame seeds

Soak the *kosari* in water for at least 24 hours, or preferably for 2 or 3 days. Drain, cut into 3−4 in (7.5−10 cm) pieces, and discard any tough stems.

Heat a frying pan with the sesame oil to medium hot. Add the *kosari*, stir well, and fry lightly. Add the soy sauce, chicken broth or water, mix well, cover, and cook for a further 10 minutes or so, or until tender and cooked through. Sprinkle with sesame seeds and serve at room temperature.

TORAJISAENGCHAE BELLFLOWER SALAD

도 라지생채

Fresh *toraji*, the white rootlets of the edible bellflower, make a delicious crunchy Korean salad, a highly prized accompaniment to any meal. Dried *toraji*, also available from Korean groceries, is the next best thing.

½ packet dried *toraji* (about 2 oz/50 g)
2 tablespoons sesame oil
1 tablespoon rice or cider vinegar
2 teaspoons sugar
2 teaspoons red pepper powder
1 garlic clove, peeled, crushed, and finely chopped
1 teaspoon toasted sesame seeds

Soak the dried *toraji* overnight, or preferably for 2 or 3 days. Drain, squeeze dry, and tear each rootlet into long, thin strips. Heat the sesame oil in a frying pan and add the *toraji*. Fry lightly for about 7−10 minutes or until soft. Add the remaining ingredients to the pan, mix well, cook for another 3 minutes. Serve at room temperature.

DRIED KOREAN RADISH *NAMUL*

무우말랭이

Though fresh Korean radish is widely available, this *namul*, made with dried radish strips, is well worth making: the dried radish has a characteristic, chewy texture, and it is eaten almost more as a condiment or relish than as a salad.

$\frac{1}{2}$ packet dried Korean radish (about 2 oz/50 g)
4 tablespoons soy sauce

---

2 tablespoons sesame oil
1 teaspoon red pepper powder
2 teaspoons sugar
2 teaspoons toasted sesame seeds

Soak the radish strips in several changes of water until softened, then tear into thin strips. Place in a bowl and soak in water overnight. The next day, drain, add the soy sauce, and mix well. Cover and leave to steep overnight, or longer.

When ready to prepare, heat the sesame oil in a frying pan, and add the radish strips in soy sauce, red pepper powder, and sugar. Stir-fry lightly for 5−7 minutes. Remove from the heat, and garnish with toasted sesame seeds.

UONGJORIM DRIED BURDOCK SALAD

우엉조림

Dried burdock is another characteristic Korean food. Like other dried roots, it is essential to soak it for considerable periods − at least two or three days, or even longer.

$\frac{1}{2}$ packet dried burdock root (about 2 oz/50 g)

$\frac{1}{4}$ lb (125 g) lean ground beef
1 tablespoon soy sauce
$\frac{1}{2}$ tablespoon sesame oil
1 garlic clove, peeled, crushed, and finely chopped

---

1 tablespoon sesame oil
2 tablespoons soy sauce
2 tablespoons broth or water
2 teaspoons sugar
2 teaspoons toasted sesame seeds

Wash the burdock root, and soak in several changes of water to soften. Cut into fine matchsticks, place in a bowl, and cover with water. Set aside for 2−3 days or longer.

When ready to prepare, marinade the ground beef in soy sauce, sesame oil, and garlic for 30 minutes. Heat the sesame oil in a frying pan, and add the beef. Fry lightly for 5 minutes, then add the drained burdock strips, soy sauce, broth or water, and sugar. Mix well, and cook for a further 7−10 minutes or until tender, and most of the liquid has been absorbed. Remove, transfer to a bowl, and garnish with the toasted sesame seeds.

Journal Notes

Korean Picnics

Everywhere we go, we see Koreans outside, picnicking families, groups of schoolchildren in bright red or yellow uniforms with matching caps and satchels, halmoni *and* haraboji *(grandmothers and grandfathers) in traditional dress, all sitting around together feasting on amazing and elaborate al fresco meals. Just as Korean meals consist of multifarious dishes, so Korean picnics are much much more than just a sandwich and a tin of drink. They are serious affairs, the picnickers transporting great wicker chests, tables, and chairs; portable burners for cooking fresh rice and soup; pots, pans and dishes; and plastic tubs full of* panchan, kimchi, *fried* jon, fish, *seaweed . . .*

Halmoni recalls that at least once a month, she and her friends from the church would have elaborate picnics at Hanauma Bay in Hawaii. It was always a communal affair, and the women prepared the foods for days beforehand. There were huge pots of raw marinaded short ribs; several different kinds of namul; kimchi, *of course, crunchy cucumber* oisobagi.

Everyone piled into whatever locomotion was available − open trucks, banana wagons, Ford coupés, an occasional Studebaker sedan. Once at the beach, the first order of the day was to get the charcoal fires going. The women started to cook the kalbi, *and the irresistible aroma of charred, marinaded short ribs drove other nearby picnickers nearly spare − the bolder approaching close enough to ask for a little taste.*

Afterwards, the children played water games while the men retired to coconut-thatched huts to play cards. But before too long, someone would begin to beat on the changgu − *hourglass drum − and two or three others would follow; hands clapped in time and several women, then more and more, would enter the circle to dance the slow, fluid Korean dances as though the music were coming from within themselves as well as from the drums.*

Finally, as the sun set over the ocean, all the remaining scraps of food would be emptied into a large cauldron set over the dying fire, for one last bowl of soup, before packing everything up and returning home.

6
Rice and Noodles

There is a casual greeting in Korean, '*Pam mogossoyo?*' which means 'Have you eaten rice?' The verb *papporihada* means to earn one's daily rice and is used where we would talk of "bread-winning". These phrases indicate the basic importance of rice, not just in the diet, but in the entire scheme of living. The rhythms of life still revolve — as they always have done — around the planting and harvesting of rice.

Our family had extensive rice estates both near Pusan and by the summer house at Sochang. Halmoni remembers the spring ritual of rice planting. Her father supervised the work, while the male servants, knee- or sometimes nearly waist-deep in mud, ploughed the fields with ox-drawn wooden ploughs, carving the wet, heavy, earth into neat furrows. Then, men and women all in a row, their baggy *paji* trousers hitched up to their waists, wearing head scarfs to guard against the sun, bent and straightened in unison, transferring the clumps of newly grown seedlings into the earth. In summer the July rains filled the paddies and fantastic Manchurian cranes and other birds came to nest in them. But if the rain and summer storms were too harsh or if there was too little rain then that year's crop could be destroyed.

In the months before the harvest, the previous season's rice had to be eked out with millet, barley, or similar grains. But finally autumn came and there was always a sense of excitement and relief in the air, as the new rice was harvested, threshed, and polished. Not only did this new season's rice taste delicious: harvest time also meant that there was money again in the house, for over three hundred bags of best quality rice were taken to Seoul to be sold.

Noodles — a symbol of longevity — are much loved by the Koreans, in common with the Japanese and Chinese. *Chapchae, kuksu*, and *naengmyon* are the three classic noodle dishes of Korea, but there are many other variations on these basic themes that are also enjoyed. Indeed, noodle stands are common in Korea and are found on many street corners though, admittedly, 'instant' noodles are as common as their fresh counterparts these days, a fact bemoaned by Uncle Donald. But still, a bowl of noodles has long been the standard and quick lunch, the most basic — and delicious — Korean fast food.

SSALBAP STEAMED WHITE RICE

쌀 밥

When my young cousin Matthew came to visit us in England, he had already been travelling around the country for a few weeks. When he sat down to dinner, he heaved a sigh of relief: 'Proper sticky Korean rice!' Korean rice is a medium-grain version, and though the grains should be well fluffed, they do indeed also stick together, making it possible to eat with pointed metal chopsticks.

Korean rice is never salted (the savouriness of the foods more than makes up for this, just as in Tuscany salty *salame* or grilled meals are balanced by bland unsalted bread). Always remember to wash rice thoroughly to remove excess starch, and to soak it before cooking. 'How long should rice be soaked?' I asked Halmoni, who flatly stated that you can't *oversoak* rice. Leave it overnight, if you want, but allow at least two or three hours.

Rice should always be measured in proportion to water, using a coffee cup or mug if you don't have a standard measuring cup.

2 cups white Korean rice
3 cups cold water

Place the rice in a pot and wash vigorously under running water for several minutes, until all the excess starch has been washed out and the water runs clear. Cover with water and leave to soak for at least 2–3 hours or longer. Drain in a sieve, then return to the pot and add the measured water. Cover tightly and bring to the boil. Stir once and immediately reduce the heat to very low. Steam for 20 minutes, or until all the water has been absorbed. Do not lift the lid while cooking.

KONGBAP RICE AND PEAS

콩 밥

Rice is without doubt the staple grain of Korea, and Koreans like to mix any number of ingredients in the rice pot, including bean sprouts, beans, chestnuts, barley, millet or sweet potatoes, as the recipes below indicate. For us, though, rice and peas have always been the family favourite, and a welcome change from plain rice. Though not strictly Korean, this is delicious with a generous pat of butter added at the end.

2 cups rice
3 cups water
1 cup fresh young peas (or substitute frozen)
Generous tablespoon butter (optional)

Place the rice in a saucepan and wash vigorously in several changes of water to remove excess starch. Leave to soak for 2–3 hours. Drain, add measured water, and bring to the boil. Stir well, cover tightly, and immediately reduce the heat to the lowest setting. After about 10 minutes add the peas and steam for a further 10–15 minutes until the rice is tender and all the water has been absorbed (if using frozen peas, adjust water accordingly). Mix the peas into the rice before serving (and add a pat of butter, if desired).

PORIBAP RICE WITH BARLEY

보 리밥

$\frac{1}{2}$ **cup pearl barley**
1$\frac{1}{2}$ cups white rice
3$\frac{1}{2}$ cups water

Soak the pearl barley for about 2 hours or longer. Wash the rice in several changes of water and soak for 2–3 hours or more. When ready to cook, drain and combine the grains in a pot, add the measured water, and bring to the boil. Stir, cover, and reduce the heat to very low. Steam for 25–30 minutes.

Brass Rice Bowls

In Halmoni's family, everybody always had their own rice bowl, as well as their own set of metal chopsticks and a metal spoon. Even when she was no more than a mere toddler, she remembers this tiny brass rice bowl, complete with lid. Her elder sisters and parents all had their own bowls, too, each a different size, marking their position in the family and coming of age, when they finally earned an adult rice bowl the size of Mother's and Father's. Each month, the house servant would gather up all the rice bowls and take them away for polishing.

I wonder, did Little Mother, Great-Grandfather's second wife, have a smaller bowl than First Mother, thus subtly signifying her lower status? Or did Great-Grandfather insist on equality? Halmoni says she cannot remember.

KIJANGBAP RICE WITH MILLET

기장밥

Before the rice harvest, at the end of the agricultural year, Halmoni remembers that the larder was almost bare, and the few remaining sacks of rice had to be eked out, stretched with the addition of millet, barley, and other grains. Even today in Seoul, many restaurants serve rice mixed with any variety of grains, not for reasons of economy, but in compliance with a government policy to support the farmers. Rice with millet, however, is worth cooking quite simply for the nutty bite and variety that this little-used grain adds.

$\frac{1}{2}$ **cup millet**
$1\frac{1}{2}$ **cups white rice**
3 cups water

Place the rice in a saucepan and wash vigorously in several changes of water to remove excess starch. Leave to soak for 2−3 hours, then drain.

Meanwhile, wash the millet and drain.

Combine the rice and millet, and add the water. Cover tightly and bring to the boil. Stir, then reduce the heat to very low and steam for about 25−30 minutes. Do not lift the lid while the rice and millet are cooking.

KONGNAMULBAP RICE WITH BEAN SPROUTS

콩 나물 밥

This is a delicious and substantial rice dish, a meal in itself together with crunchy *namul* and a saucer of *kimchi*.

2 cups rice
$\frac{1}{2}$ **lb (250 g) soy bean sprouts**
$\frac{1}{4}$ **lb (125 g) beef**
2 tablespoons soy sauce
1 tablespoon sesame oil
2 spring onions, finely chopped
2 garlic cloves, peeled, crushed, and finely chopped
2 tablespoons toasted sesame seeds
1 tablespoon vegetable oil
3 cups water
Salt

Place the rice in a saucepan and wash vigorously in several changes of water to remove excess starch. Leave to soak for 2−3 hours, then drain. Wash the soy bean sprouts and trim off their fine hairlike roots. Slice the beef into thin strips. Mix together the soy sauce, sesame oil, spring onions, garlic, and toasted sesame seeds, and add to the meat. Leave to marinade for 30 minutes.

Heat a little vegetable oil in a large pot. Stir-fry the beef briefly until brown. Add the rice and bean sprouts, stir to mix well, then pour on the water. Cover and bring to the boil. Stir once more, then reduce heat to a bare simmer. Cook for 25−30 minutes. When ready, mix the rice, bean sprouts, and beef together before serving.

PAMBAP RICE WITH CHESTNUTS

밤 밥

When my mother was sent out to Korea as a tiny baby, she was so ill from the journey and the change in water and diet that she almost died. She was saved, though, by chestnuts, boiled and mashed to a purée — all that she could eat. Even today, her favourite food — her desert island food if she were allowed only one — is *marron glacé*. This humble dish may be somewhat less elegant than the European speciality, but it is delicious nonetheless.

2 cups white rice
4 oz (125 g) chestnuts, boiled, shelled, and skinned
$3\frac{1}{2}$ cups water

Place the rice in a saucepan and wash vigorously in several changes of water to remove excess starch. Leave to soak for 2−3 hours, then drain. Cut the peeled, cooked chestnuts into quarters and combine with the rice. Add the water, cover tightly, and bring to the boil. Stir once, then reduce the heat to very low and steam for about 25−30 minutes. Do not lift the lid while the rice is cooking. When ready, fluff and mix with a fork.

PATBAP RICE WITH BEANS

팟 밥

This is a good easy rice dish for winter, hearty and filling. The combination of rice and beans reminds me of one of my other favourite cuisines, Mexican.

2 cups rice
$\frac{1}{2}$ cup red beans
$3\frac{1}{2}$ cups liquid (a mixture of water and bean liquid)

Place the rice in a saucepan and wash vigorously in several changes of water to remove excess starch. Leave to soak for 2−3 hours, then drain. Soak the beans for 2 hours, then cook until tender, about 30−45 minutes. Drain, reserving the cooking liquid. Mix the uncooked rice and the cooked beans together in a pot. Add the liquid (the reserved bean liquid made up with water). Cover tightly and bring to the boil. Stir once, reduce heat to very low, and steam for 25−30 minutes.

PIBIMBAP MIXED RICE WITH VEGETABLES

비빔밥

Pibimbap is one of the classics of the Korean table, yet it is really a simple one-dish meal, a mixture of rice and any assortment of cooked cultivated and wild vegetables, perhaps some meat, a fried egg, or even a piece of watermelon. Add a generous dollop of *kochujang*, stir the whole mixture vigorously, then tuck in with a spoon.

Chonju *pibimbap*, from that southern city in the Cholla province, is reputed to be the finest variation of this national favourite. What is most striking about *pibimbap* Chonju-style is that it is invariably served in massive stone bowls which are heated over a bare flame so that the mixture arrives still sizzling and cooking. You have to keep turning it and mixing it with a spoon and the bottom layer of rice develops a most appetizing and delicious crust. Moreover, *pibimbap* — or anything else eaten in Cholla-do, is invariably accompanied by an astonishing array of *panchan*, the table literally covered with bowls of delicious side dishes.

If you don't have any *toraji* or *kosari*, then substitute other vegetables such as cooked and dressed spinach or watercress, or steamed carrot strips.

4 cups freshly cooked white rice

$\frac{1}{4}$lb (125 g) beef, thinly sliced
2 tablespoons soy sauce
1 tablespoon sesame oil
1 teaspoon toasted sesame seeds
1 garlic clove, peeled, crushed, and finely chopped
$\frac{1}{2}$in (12 mm) piece of fresh ginger, peeled, crushed, and finely chopped
2 spring onions, finely chopped
Freshly ground black pepper

$\frac{1}{2}$lb (125 g) soy bean or mung bean sprouts
1 tablespoon sesame oil
1 spring onion, shredded on the diagonal
1 garlic clove, peeled, crushed, and finely chopped
1 teaspoon toasted sesame seeds

---

1 cucumber
1 teaspoon salt
1 teaspoon rice vinegar
$\frac{1}{2}$ teaspoon sesame oil

1 spring onion, finely chopped
½ teaspoon toasted sesame seeds

---

2 oz (50 g) *kosarinamul*, cooked and prepared (see p. 94)
2 oz (50 g) *torajinamul*, cooked and prepared (see p. 95)
2 sheets *kimgui*, cut into strips (see p. 46)
2–4 raw eggs
2 tablespoons toasted sesame seeds
Kochujang to taste

Mix the beef with the seasonings and leave to marinade for about 30 minutes. Then stir-fry for about 5 minutes until cooked. Set aside.

Wash the bean sprouts and trim off their fine roots. Plunge them into boiling water, and cook quickly until tender. Drain and squeeze out the excess water. Add the seasonings and stir-fry for about 30 seconds, then set aside.

Thinly slice the cucumber. Add the salt, and cover with cold water. Set aside for an hour, then drain and rinse in fresh water. Squeeze out excess moisture. Add the seasonings.

To serve, heat 2–4 ovenproof bowls in the oven until very hot. Add the cooked rice to these bowls. Arrange the beef, bean sprouts, cucumber, prepared *kosari* and *toraji* in an attractive alternate pattern on the rice. Break a raw egg on top of the pile, and decorate with shredded strips of *kimgui* and toasted sesame seeds. To eat, add *kochujang* to taste, mix thoroughly, and eat with a spoon together with *kimchi* and *namul*.

OGOKBAP FIVE-GRAIN RICE

오곡밥

Though in other cases rice may have been mixed with other grains to stretch it, this dish is by no means a poor person's rice, but a very special and splendid one. The recipe below makes a large pot to serve as a party centre-piece; scale it down if necessary, and experiment with other grains and beans.

$\frac{1}{4}$ cup black beans
$\frac{1}{4}$ cup red beans
$\frac{1}{4}$ cup pearl barley
$\frac{1}{4}$ cup millet
1 cup rice
$\frac{1}{2}$ cup glutinous rice

Soak the black beans and red beans in plenty of water for about 3 or 4 hours. Soak the barley and millet for 2 hours. Wash the rices thoroughly and soak for 2−3 hours or longer. Cook the red and black beans in water for 30−45 minutes, or until tender. Drain and set aside, reserving the cooking liquid. In a deep, heavy pot, add the cooked beans, the soaked barley, millet, and drained rices. Add $3\frac{1}{2}$ cups liquid (bean cooking liquid made up with water). Bring to the boil, stir to mix the grains well, and reduce to a simmer. Cover tightly and cook for 30 minutes.

POSOTBAP RICE WITH MUSHROOMS

버섯밥

Another fairly substantial rice dish that is suitable for a lunch or light supper. Though Koreans are unanimous in their passion for white rice, we think that brown rice makes this dish even nuttier and tastier.

2 cups brown rice
$\frac{1}{2}$ lb (250 g) mushrooms, washed and sliced
$\frac{1}{4}$ lb (125 g) lean ground beef
2 spring onions, finely chopped
2 tablespoons soy sauce
$\frac{1}{2}$ tablespoon sesame oil
1 tablespoon toasted sesame seeds
Plenty of freshly ground black pepper

1 tablespoon vegetable oil
3 cups water

Place the rice in a saucepan and wash. Leave to soak for 1—2 hours, then drain. Mix together the sliced mushrooms, ground beef, spring onions, soy sauce, sesame oil, sesame seeds, and plenty of black pepper. Leave to marinade for 30 minutes. Heat a little oil in a pot, fry the meat and mushroom mixture briefly, then add the soaked and drained rice and the water. Cover with a lid, bring to the boil, stir, then reduce to a simmer. Cook for 30— 35 minutes. Stir well before serving.

Chonju Paper

Chonju, a fine and leisurely old provincial town, is noted not only for its *pibimbap* and other gastronomic delights, but also for its fine paper and paper artefacts. Paper has been made in Korea for at least a thousand years and has been highly regarded by native, Chinese, and Japanese calligraphers. But this is far more than a mere surface for writing or painting on: here it is used as a flooring material; it covers the lattice-work of doors and windows, keeping out the harsh winter cold; it covers the walls; and of course paper is used to make fans, umbrellas, hats, and much else.

The finest paper is still made traditionally by hand, from any number of types of wood and bark, each with its own special properties and qualities. We saw mulberry paper being made at the Korean Folk Village and it is a fascinating process to watch: the boiled, bleached, and pounded bark is mixed with water to make a thin, fibrous pulp. This is contained in a wooden trough over which a bamboo sieve is suspended. The paper maker, with a skilled and deft movement of the arms and wrists, scoops out the pulp, rocks the sieve back and forth, spreading the pulp into a thin layer, squeezes out the excess water, then deposits a still wet, ragged-edged sheet of paper on to a pile. Afterwards, each piece of paper is dried separately. Wonder at its softness, its whiteness, and its thin consistency. The making of paper seems to me a near miraculous achievement yet it is one which we take for granted every day.

KUKSU KOREAN 'SPAGHETTI'

국 수

I love noodles — any kind of noodles. But what I love best of all is a big bowl full of *kuksu*: Korean 'spaghetti', swimming in home-made broth and garnished with *pulgogi* or pork, strips of egg, sharp vinegary cucumbers and dressed spinach or watercress *namul*. This is the way my mother makes this family favourite.

1 lb (500 g) steak (alternatively pork or chicken can be used)
2 garlic cloves, peeled, crushed, and finely chopped
1 in (2.5 cm) piece of fresh ginger, peeled, crushed, and finely chopped
2 tablespoons soy sauce
1 tablespoon sesame oil
2 teaspoons sesame seeds
1 teaspoon sugar
Freshly ground black pepper

---

2 cucumbers
3 tablespoons salt
3 tablespoons cider vinegar
1 tablespoon sugar
1 teaspoon red pepper powder

---

1 lb (500 g) spinach or 2 bunches watercress, washed and trimmed
2 tablespoons soy sauce
1 tablespoon sesame oil
1 tablespoon toasted sesame seeds

---

1 lb (500 g) *son myon* (Korean vermicelli)
About 4 pints (2 litres) homemade beef broth

---

3 spring onions, shredded on the diagonal
4 eggs, beaten, fried one at a time, and cut into thin strips

Slice the beef across the grain into thin strips (if using pork or chicken, cut into thin strips). Mix together the marinade ingredients and add to the meat. Leave to marinade for 30 minutes. Fry for about 5–7 minutes, or until cooked through (longer for chicken and pork).

Thinly slice the cucumbers. Add the salt and cover with water. Set aside for 30 minutes, then rinse well, drain, and squeeze out excess moisture. Dress with vinegar, sugar, and red pepper powder.

Steam the spinach (or watercress) briefly, and squeeze out

excess moisture. Chop coarsely and dress with soy sauce, sesame oil, and toasted sesame seeds.

Heat up the homemade broth. Bring another pot of water to the boil. Add the noodles and cook for 3 minutes only or until cooked through but still *al dente*. Drain and rinse thoroughly under running water to remove excess starch.

To serve, place sufficient noodles in each bowl and add enough broth to come up about halfway in the bowl. Garnish with the fried meat, marinaded cucumbers, dressed spinach, egg strips, and shredded spring onions.

PIBIMGUKSU COLD NOODLES WITH VEGETABLES

비빔국수

Uncle Larry remembers *pibimguksu* from childhood days in Hawaii, a hot brimming bowl full of *son myon* noodles garnished with vegetables and meat. But we prefer this tasty and refreshing cold version that we ate many times for lunch during our travels.

1 lb (500 g) *son myon* noodles

2 tablespoons *kochujang*
1 tablespoon vinegar
1 tablespoon sesame oil
2 garlic cloves, peeled, crushed, and finely chopped
2 teaspoons toasted sesame seeds

2 carrots, peeled and cut into thin matchsticks
1 in (2.5 cm) piece of fresh ginger, peeled and cut into thin matchsticks
6 spring onions, shredded finely on the diagonal
4 slices cooked ham, cut into thin matchsticks
2 oz (50 g) Chinese cabbage, finely shredded
4 eggs, beaten, fried one at a time, and cut into thin strips

Bring a pot of water to the boil. Add the noodles and cook for 3–4 minutes only or until cooked through but still *al dente*. Drain and rinse thoroughly under running water to remove excess starch. Chill well.

Mix together the *kochujang*, vinegar, sesame oil, garlic, and toasted sesame seeds.

To serve, divide the noodles into 4 bowls. Add a tablespoon of sauce to each, then top with the carrots, ginger, spring onions, ham, cabbage, and egg strips. Mix well before eating.

NAENGMYON COLD BUCKWHEAT NOODLES

냉 면

Cold *naengmyon* — chewy brown buckwheat noodles — swimming in a sharp, vinegary broth, garnished with boiled beef and crunchy slices of Korean pear is a delicious and refreshing summer classic.

1½ lb (750 g) beef for boiling (rump or brisket)
3 tablespoons soy sauce
1 garlic clove, peeled, crushed, and finely chopped
1 tablespoon sesame oil
1 tablespoon toasted sesame seeds
Freshly ground black pepper

---

2 eggs, hard boiled
1 Korean pear, peeled and cored (if not available then do not substitute)

---

1 cucumber, thinly sliced
1 tablespoon salt
1 tablespoon cider or rice vinegar
½ tablespoon sugar
½ teaspoon red pepper powder

---

1 lb (500 g) buckwheat noodles
2 tablespoons *kimchi* juice
6 tablespoons rice or cider vinegar
1 tablespoon sugar
Salt
1 tablespoon vinegar mustard sauce (see p. 36)

Bring about 3 pints (1½ litres) water to the boil and add the beef. Skim several times then simmer for 1–1½ hours or until tender. Allow the meat to cool in the broth, then remove and slice. Mix the sliced meat with the soy sauce, garlic, sesame oil, sesame seeds, and black pepper. Allow the broth to cool and skim off any fat from the surface. Mix the broth with the *kimchi* juice and vinegar and season with salt to taste. Chill this broth and the meat in the refrigerator until ready to serve.

Cut the hard-boiled eggs in half lengthwise. Core the Korean pear (if using) and cut into slices.

Add the salt to sliced cucumber, cover with water, and set aside for 30 minutes. Rinse well, drain, and squeeze out excess moisture. Mix with vinegar, sugar, and red pepper powder.

Bring a large pot of water to the boil and cook the buckwheat noodles for 3—5 minutes until cooked (they should be still *al dente* but not too tough or overly elastic). Drain, then rinse well in cold water.

To serve, add noodles to each bowl. Add chilled broth mixture about halfway up each bowl. Top with a few slices of beef, the marinaded cucumber, a slice of Korean pear (if using) and half a hard-boiled egg. Add a few ice cubes to the bowl to keep it really well chilled. Serve with vinegar mustard sauce.

Journal Notes

Sister and Scissors: Noodle Protocol

Michele went out on a date one night last spring to a Korean restaurant near where she lives. 'Don't forget to try the naengmyon,*' I suggested, as I knew the cold buckwheat noodles are generally quite good. When she returned, I asked how it had all gone. She could not stop giggling.*

'Are the noodles supposed to be so tough that you can't eat them?' she asked. 'Not really,' I replied. 'Well, these were,' she continued. 'I couldn't even chew them with my teeth, they were so rubbery. My friend thought it was hilarious and suggested I ask for some scissors. The Korean woman who runs the place must have heard me, for in a moment, she returned with a huge pair of shears and snip-snipped like a madwoman, furiously cutting the noodles into small pieces. Then she disappeared. I hope I didn't offend her.'

This did indeed sound like rather bizarre and unreasonable behaviour on the part of the restaurateur. However, when we went out for noodles in Seoul, we found that there the waitresses all carry scissors as a matter of course, and will gladly snip-snip the naengmyon, kuksu *and other noodles whenever customers so desire. So, Michele was relieved to find, that seeming madwoman had simply thought that she — Michele — was au fait with Korean noodle protocol.*

CHAPCHAE VERMICELLI NOODLES WITH VEGETABLES

잡 채

Chapchae, according to Halmoni, is one of those dishes that you always have at a Korean party. When she and her friends had gatherings at Hanauma Bay, or Waikiki, or Ala Moana, someone always brought along a big pot of this noodle and vegetable dish, a sort of Korean chop-suey. *Chapchae* is delicious even cold, but I like it best piping hot.

Marinade
2 garlic cloves, peeled, crushed, and finely chopped
1 in (2.5 cm) piece of fresh ginger, peeled, crushed, and finely chopped
$\frac{1}{4}$ pint (150 ml) soy sauce
3 tablespoons sesame oil
1 tablespoon toasted sesame seeds
Plently of freshly ground black pepper
1 tablespoon sugar

---

4 thin pork chops, trimmed and cut into thin matchsticks
1 oz (30 g) Chinese mushrooms, cleaned, trimmed and soaked for 3−4 hours
$\frac{1}{2}$ oz (15 g) *mogi posot* mushrooms, cleaned and soaked (optional)
2 carrots, peeled, and cut into matchsticks
1 large tin bamboo shoots, cut into matchsticks
Sesame oil for frying
1 onion, peeled, cut in half lengthwise, then into thin slices
$\frac{1}{2}$ packet *tang myon* (Korean sweet potato vermicelli), about $\frac{1}{2}$ lb (250 g); or if not available then substitute Chinese rice vermicelli

---

1 in (2.5 cm) piece of fresh ginger, peeled, and cut into thin matchsticks
1 tablespoon toasted sesame seeds
2 eggs, beaten, fried, and sliced into thin strips
2 oz *pulgogi* or roast pork, cut into thin matchsticks to garnish
4 spring onions, shredded on the diagonal

Mix together the marinade ingredients. Place the meat and mushrooms in a bowl together with half the marinade. Mix well with the hands, and set aside for about 30 minutes.

When ready to prepare, heat the sesame oil in large frying pan and stir-fry the prepared carrots and bamboo shoots for a few minutes. Then add a few spoonfuls of marinade and continue to cook slowly for a further 5 minutes until the vegetables have softened, but remain crisp (add more marinade while cooking if necessary). Transfer to a large pot.

In the same frying pan, add a little more sesame oil and quickly fry the meat and mushrooms in small batches, transferring to the pot when done.

Finally, fry the sliced onions together with the remaining marinade for 1 or 2 minutes only (depending on how sweet the onions are). They, too, should remain crisp.

Meanwhile, have a large pot of water boiling on the stove. Add *tang myon* or rice vermicelli and cook according to the instructions on the packet, (usually about 5 minutes or so for *tang myon*, much less for rice vermicelli). The noodles should remain *al dente*. Drain, rinse off excess starch if necessary, and add the noodles to the pot with the meat and vegetables. Add the matchsticks of ginger and the toasted sesame seeds. Mix well. Garnish with egg strips, strips of *pulgogi* or roast pork, and shredded spring onions.

KONGJORIM SOY-GLAZED BLACK BEANS
콩 조 림

Sweet and savoury black soy beans are served as a side dish to be eaten as a condiment, another example of the Korean penchant for salty, sweet, and savoury nibbles.

6 oz (175 g) black soy beans
3 tablespoons sugar
3 tablespoons soy sauce
1 tablespoon sesame oil
2 teaspoons toasted sesame seeds

Wash the beans and soak in water for 4–6 hours or longer. Rinse well and drain, then place in a pot. Cover with water, bring to the boil and simmer until just tender. Drain, return to a clean pot, and add sugar, soy sauce, and sesame oil. Mix well and cook over a fairly high heat, stirring frequently until the beans are well glazed and soft. Garnish with toasted sesame seeds.

PIBIMNAENGMYON BUCKWHEAT NOODLES WITH
CHILLI SAUCE

비빔냉면

There are hot foods, and there are *hot* foods: *pibimnaengmyon* is definitely in the latter category: a bowlful of lukewarm buckwheat noodles, served with a super-hot chilli sauce, together with a few slices of boiled meat, hard-boiled egg, and Korean radish. The heat, moreover, is deceptive, and sneaks up on you not all at once, but only after you have eaten half the bowl, and thus past the point of no return. So have plenty of iced water on hand (or don't add the extra red pepper powder to the sauce). This spicy speciality, for some reason, seems to be always served with a cup of hot beef broth on the side, but, believe me, this does little to cool you down. Even still, I can never resist it.

1 lb (500 g) *naengmyon* (buckwheat noodles)

---

2 tablespoons *kochujang*
2—4 teaspoons red pepper powder, or to taste
1 tablespoon rice or cider vinegar
1 tablespoon sesame oil
3 garlic cloves, peeled, crushed, and finely chopped
2 teaspoons toasted sesame seeds
2 teaspoons sugar
3 spring onions, finely chopped

½ lb (250 g) boiled beef, sliced (see p. 110)
2 eggs, hard boiled
1 Korean radish, peeled, and sliced (if available, use slices of *tong chimi*)

1½ pints (900 ml) homemade beef broth

Bring a large pot of water to the boil and cook the buckwheat noodles for 3—5 minutes until cooked (they should be still *al dente* but not too tough or overly elastic). Drain, then rinse well in cold water and set aside.

Mix together the sauce ingredients: *kochujang*, red pepper powder to taste, vinegar, oil, garlic, sesame seeds, sugar, and spring onions.

To serve, place a portion of cooked lukewarm noodles in each bowl, and top with a generous spoonful of the chilli sauce, followed by a slice or two of boiled beef, a slice of Korean radish or *tong chimi*, and half a hard-boiled egg. Mix well before eating. Serve with a cup or mug of beef broth on the side.

7
Meat and Poultry

As a young girl growing up in southeast Korea, Halmoni had never seen a pig. Pork simply was not eaten but beef, in particular, as well as chicken, were popular mainstays, together with fish, rice, and vegetables. Today pigs are a common sight throughout the country, but Korea remains, on the whole, a nation of beef eaters. Such dishes as *pulgogi*, *kalbi*, or *yukhoe* are certainly convincing demonstrations of Korean expertise in beef preparation.

Yet for some reason, butchers in Korea have traditionally been considered social outcasts, together with willow workers and tanners. Such *paekchong* were often forced to live outside the community in their own separate hamlets. But here too, there was a pecking order: beef butchers were superior to pork butchers.

Once, Halmoni remembers, a family of butchers tried to move into Sochang, her village. When they were cast out by the villagers, they bivouacked in a disused waterwheel beside a stream at the bottom of her father's estate. Halmoni's father was a kind man who, when he discovered them, allowed them to stay, although the villagers objected. Halmoni remembers them well: often, she says, one of the children would bring choice morsels of meat to her father out of gratitude. They were still living there when she left for Pusan and later Hawaii.

I wonder why, in a nation of hearty meat-eaters, butchers should be so despised. Apparently regarded as outcasts as far back as the Koryo dynasty, a time when Buddhism was the state religion, I can only imagine that Buddhist strictures on meat eating are the cause.

PULGOGI / KOREAN BARBECUED BEEF

불고기

Pulgogi is probably the best-known and most popular of all Korean foods. In restaurants, it is often prepared theatrically at the table on a brass or iron shield. However, cooked over a *hibachi* barbecue, grilled, or fried in a very hot frying pan, it is always delicious and a family favourite.

2 lb (1 kg) sirloin steak

Marinade
5 tablespoons soy sauce
3 garlic cloves, peeled, crushed, and finely chopped
1 in (2.5 cm) piece of fresh ginger, peeled, crushed, and finely chopped
2 tablespoons sesame oil
2 teaspoons sugar
Freshly ground black pepper
4 spring onions, sliced
1 tablespoon toasted sesame seeds

---

1 lettuce
***Kochujang* to taste (optional)**

If necessary, score the meat and pound lightly with a meat hammer to tenderize. Slice the meat into thin strips across the grain on the diagonal bias. Combine the marinade ingredients and add to the meat. Mix well with the hands, then set aside for at least 1 hour.

Prepare a charcoal fire if using. Remove the meat from the marinade and grill over the hot coals for 5—7 minutes, turning with tongs frequently.

Alternatively, if you have a domed shield, place this over the fire, allow to heat up, then place the meat strips on the hot metal, turning as required. The meat may also be cooked under a hot grill, or fried in a very hot frying pan.

Serve with steamed white rice together with a pile of cleaned lettuce leaves and the *kochujang* if desired. Either eat as it is, or else take a lettuce leaf, add a bit of rice, some strips of meat and a little dab of *kochujang*. Roll up to make packets to eat with the fingers.

PULGOGI II KOREAN BARBECUED BEEF

불고기

Pulgogi, of course, is a favourite that we have always loved, and all of us have our own slightly different ways of preparing it. This is my mother's version, differing from the previous, classic version primarily in the fact that the meat is not cut into strips, but rather is scored deeply and left in larger pieces. This method is perhaps more suited to cooking on an outside barbecue rather than on a domed shield.

2 lb (1 kg) sirloin or flank steak

Marinade
3 garlic cloves, peeled and finely chopped
1 in (2.5 cm) piece of fresh ginger, peeled, and finely chopped
3 tablespoons soy sauce
1 tablespoon vinegar
1 tablespoon vegetable oil
2 teaspoons toasted sesame seeds
5 or 6 spring onions, sliced
1 heaped teaspoon sugar
Plenty of freshly ground black pepper

Score the meat very deeply (nearly through to the other side) in a criss-cross diamond pattern. Turn over and score on the other side (don't worry if it breaks up into two or three pieces). Pound lightly with the back of a knife or a meat hammer to tenderize.

Mix together all the marinade ingredients and add to the meat. Mix well with the hands, then leave for 30 minutes or longer.

Meanwhile, prepare a charcoal fire and wait until the coals are at their hottest (white). Cook over hot coals, turning only once. *Pulgogi* must cook very quickly. Alternatively, grill or fry over the hottest flame possible.

Journal Notes

Paegam Hot Springs

After a few days walking in the Sorak mountains, we drove all the way down the East Coast today, a breathtaking journey past wide sandy beaches, terraced rice paddies, and tiny fishing hamlets, the roofs of the houses creating a motley pattern of blue, turquoise, and orange. It was a long drive, we were all tired and were glad when we arrived at Paegam, famous for its natural hot springs. We immediately repaired to a public bath house.

Korean bath houses are amazing institutions. They existed traditionally in the days when most houses had no private bathing facilities, but they are much more than places simply to clean yourself. Strictly segregated, they are great and egalitarian temples to pleasure and pure relaxation. They are certainly not for the shy, or for those who are pressed for time.

I entered the steaming bath area, and first took a shower and washed myself — the ultimate faux pas, apparently, is to enter the bath itself and wash there. Only once cleansed did I dare venture into the spring tub itself. The temperature at first was excruciating. After a minute or two it was still painful but I did finally succumb to a rather numbing senselessness as I sat on the stone edge of the ontang, *luxuriating in the steam, and watching all the activity around me. When I'd had enough, I took a plunge in the icy* naengtang *or cold tank, then repaired to a little foot shower to scrub down further. Repeated visits to the* ontang *were interspersed with plunges in the* naengtang, *but the* yoltang, *a super-hot tank, nearly killed me it was so hot.*

After repeated trips around the circuit, I moved on to the next room where I dried myself, combed my hair, utilized every potion and after-shave in front of me (as everyone else seemed to be doing). Finally, I put on a clean robe and slippers and went out to a central bar area where I was served with OB maekchu *and peanuts.*

KALBIGUI BARBECUED SHORT RIBS

갈비구이

The same basic marinade that is used for *pulgogi* is also delicious on beef short ribs, another Korean classic. Though this cut is not too well-known in Britain, a good butcher will prepare it for you. Choose good, meaty ribs and have the butcher cut them into two inch pieces. Though the meat may be just scored in a diamond pattern, we like *kalbi* best when the meat is laid back from the bone, marinaded, and charcoal grilled over hot coals. In *kalbigui* in Korea, this speciality would be cooked over charcoal or a gas flame directly at your table.

2 lb (1 kg) beef short ribs, cut into 2 in (5 cm) pieces

Marinade
4 tablespoons soy sauce
1½ tablespoons sesame oil
4 garlic cloves, peeled, crushed, and finely chopped
1 in (2.5 cm) piece of fresh ginger, peeled, crushed, and finely chopped
4 spring onions, shredded on the diagonal
1 tablespoon toasted sesame seeds
2 teaspoons sugar
Freshly ground black pepper

While keeping the meat attached to the bone of the short ribs, slice it away on one side in 1 or 2 layers to lay it away 'butterfly' fashion. Score deeply in a diamond pattern (it doesn't matter if some of the meat becomes detached from the bone). Place the ribs in a large bowl, mix all the marinade ingredients together, and pour over the meat. Leave to stand for at least 3–4 hours, or preferably overnight.

Prepare a charcoal fire and when the coals are white hot, cook the ribs until the fat is crisp and charred, about 5–7 minutes a side. If not cooking over charcoal, cook under a hot grill. Serve while piping hot, together with rice, *kimchi*, and salads.

CHANGJORIM KOREAN 'HOT MEAT'

장조림

Koreans love strongly flavoured foods, but usually they are eaten in rather small quantities, almost as a condiment to accompany great quantities of steamed white rice. For this dish, choose a gelatinous cut of meat, like shin or chuck, so that when chilled, the hot soy sauce mixture becomes a tasty jelly. We like our hot meat really hot. Experiment with the amount of chillies used.

> **2 lb (1 kg) beef shin or chuck**
> **About 10 fresh green or red chillies, or to taste**
> **6 tablespoons soy sauce**
> **3 tablespoons sesame oil**
> **1 green pepper, seeded and cut into strips**
> **$\frac{1}{2}$ pint (300 ml) water**

Place the meat, chillies, soy sauce, sesame oil, green pepper strips, and water in a large pot. Bring to the simmer and cook, partially covered, over a very slow flame for 2−3 hours or until the meat is tender to the point of falling apart. Remove from the heat and cool in the liquid. Break up the meat with a fork, and serve in a bowl with the chillies, pepper, and soy sauce jelly (the liquid should set when chilled). 'Hot meat' is eaten in small quantities as a side dish with rice, *kimchi*, and other *panchan*.

Fire Cooking

As descendants of the Mongol tribes, Koreans − even in this modern age − still love most of all foods cooked over an open or charcoal fire. In restaurants all over the country, waitresses come to your table swinging great buckets of white-hot coals which they plunk in a well in the centre of the table.

Otherwise, restaurants have gas pipes laid to each table or use small portable table-top burners for direct cooking. In the better restaurants, elaborate fans and vents absorb the fumes and smoke that arise from meats such as *pulgogi* cooked on brass-domed shields and *kalbi* − meaty short ribs − laid out on metal grids. Other foods prepared at the table over burners include *chongol* (a mixture of meats and/or seafood and vegetables cooked in a broth) and *chaengban* (boiled brisket, vegetables, noodles, and dumplings prepared in a flattish dish).

For my taste, there is nothing comparable to the immediate pleasure of eating food fire-cooked at the table.

TUNGSHIMGUI KOREAN-STYLE BARBECUED SIRLOIN

등심구이

Thinly sliced sirloin steak, rubbed lightly with crushed garlic, seasoned with nothing else but sesame oil, toasted sesame seeds and salt, then cooked over hot coals: simple and delicious.

1 large sirloin steak (about 1½ lb/750 g)
1 garlic clove, peeled and lightly crushed
2 tablespoons sesame oil
1 tablespoon toasted sesame seeds
Sea salt

Trim the steak, then cut across the grain on the slant into thin slices. Rub each slice lightly with the crushed garlic, then season with sesame oil, toasted sesame seeds, and a little sea salt.

Cook the steak slices over charcoal or under a hot grill for only a minute or two each side.

SOEGOGIGOCHUBOKKUM STIR-FRY BEEF AND CHILLIES

쇠고기고추볶음

A quick and simple, delicious stir-fry.

½ lb (250 g) sirloin steak
1 tablespoon soy sauce
3 garlic cloves, peeled, crushed, and finely chopped
1 teaspoon sugar
1 tablespoon rice wine or dry sherry
Plenty of freshly ground black pepper
About 6–8 red or green fresh chillies
1 tablespoon vegetable oil
2 teaspoons toasted sesame seeds

Slice the beef into thin strips and mix with the soy sauce, garlic, sugar, wine, and pepper. Set aside to marinade for about 1 hour.

Remove the seeds from the chillies and cut into very thin strips. Heat the oil in a frying pan and stir-fry the chillies briefly (about 2 minutes). Transfer to a dish. Stir-fry the seasoned beef for about 4–5 minutes. Return the chillies to the pan, mix well, and stir-fry again for another few minutes. Transfer to a platter, sprinkle with toasted sesame seeds and serve at once.

KALBI-TCHIM BRAISED SHORT RIBS

갈비찜

We think that the old adage that meat is sweeter near the bone is a true one, particularly in the case of short ribs. *Kalbi-tchim* is another Korean classic: short ribs slowly braised in soy sauce and wine until the meat is gooey and delicious, almost falling off the bone.

3 lb (1.5 kg) beef short ribs, cut into 2 in (5 cm) lengths
6 tablespoons soy sauce
2 tablespoons sesame oil
3 garlic cloves, peeled, crushed, and finely chopped
1 in (2.5 cm) piece of fresh ginger, peeled, crushed, and finely chopped
4 spring onions, finely chopped
3 tablespoons sugar
2 tablespoons toasted sesame seeds
4 tablespoons cooking wine (rice wine or dry sherry)
Freshly ground black pepper

1 onion, peeled and cut into large chunks
2 carrots, peeled and roughly chopped
Water
3 tablespoons pine nuts
2 teaspoons toasted sesame seeds
1 egg, beaten, fried, and cut into thin strips

Trim the excess fat from the short ribs and score in a diamond pattern. Mix the soy sauce, sesame oil, garlic, ginger, spring onions, sugar, toasted sesame seeds, wine, and black pepper together. Add to the ribs and mix thoroughly. Set aside for 3—4 hours, or overnight.

Remove the ribs from the marinade and reserve. Heat a tablespoon of vegetable oil in a large pot, and fry the ribs until brown, about 5—7 minutes. Add the onion and carrots, and fry for 2—3 minutes. Pour the reserved marinade plus $\frac{1}{2}$ pint (300 ml) of water over the meat and vegetables. Bring to the boil, and partially cover. Reduce to a low simmer and cook for $1\frac{1}{2}$—2 hours, turning the ribs from time to time, until they are very tender.

Remove the lid and boil fiercely to reduce the liquid to a thickish syrup. Make sure that all the ribs are well glazed. Skim off excess fat, and garnish with pine nuts, toasted sesame seeds, and fried egg strips. Serve piping hot.

(*Note*: This dish is even better if you cook it a day in advance, allow the pot to cool, skim off the excess fat, then reheat before serving.)

PYONYUK BOILED PRESSED BRISKET OF BEEF

편 육

I love boiled foods! Whether Austrian *tafelspitz*, Italian *bollito misto*, or this simple Korean boiled brisket, *pyonyuk*, there is something always so satisfying and basic about foods simply cooked in boiling water. Brisket, though an inexpensive cut, is one of our favourites for it is always full of flavour. Eat this meat at room temperature, like a salad, dressed with vinegar soy sauce.

---

2 lb (1 kg) beef brisket

---

2 carrots
1 cucumber
2 eggs, hard boiled

---

4 tablespoons soy sauce
1 tablespoon rice or cider vinegar
1 garlic clove, peeled, crushed, and finely chopped
2 spring onions, finely chopped
2 teaspoons toasted sesame seeds
Freshly ground black pepper

Bring a large pot of water to a vigorous boil, then add the piece of brisket. Allow to boil for 2–3 minutes to seal, then reduce the heat to a bare simmer. Cook until tender, about $1-1\frac{1}{2}$ hours. Reserve the beef broth for other soup or noodle dishes. Wrap the meat in a piece of cheesecloth or muslin, place in a flat dish with a plate or board over it, and cover with a heavy weight to press. Leave until cool, then transfer to a refrigerator until the meat is firm (2–3 hours or overnight).

Slice the carrots and the cucumber on the diagonal. Slice the hard-boiled eggs.

When ready to serve, trim the brisket of excess fat and gristle, then cut into thin slices. Arrange in overlapping slices on a platter, together with the carrots, cucumber, and eggs.

Mix together the soy sauce, vinegar, garlic, spring onions, sesame seeds, and black pepper. Pour this sauce over the meat and vegetables.

SHINSOLLO KOREAN ROYAL HOT-POT

신선로

Imagine: a dish so special that a century ago it could only be prepared for and eaten by royalty! This is *shinsollo*, an exotic medley of meat, chicken, fish, vegetables, eggs, pine and gingko nuts, all cooked separately then braised together in a rich broth in a special charcoal-fired chafing dish. This is a classic example of refined Yi dynasty palace cooking; indeed, Halmoni says that she learned how to prepare this speciality from an old lady in Hawaii who was once actually a cook for the last royal household.

Shinsollo does take a long time to prepare: but it really is worth it. If you can't get a special *shinsollo* pot from a Korean grocer, Mongolian hot pots available from Chinese shops may be used instead. Or else improvise with an attractive ovenproof serving pot.

$\frac{1}{4}$lb (125 g) sirloin steak
$\frac{1}{4}$lb (125 g) skinless chicken breast
$\frac{1}{4}$lb (125 g) skinless white fish fillets
$\frac{1}{4}$lb (125 g) calves' liver

Salt
Freshly ground black pepper
4 tablespoons flour
2 eggs, beaten
Vegetable oil for frying

$\frac{1}{4}$lb (125 g) lean ground beef
1 spring onion, finely chopped
$\frac{1}{2}$in (12 mm) piece of fresh ginger, peeled, and finely chopped
2 teaspoons soy sauce
$\frac{1}{2}$ garlic clove, peeled, crushed, and finely chopped

---

$\frac{1}{4}$lb (125 g) bean sprouts
4 Chinese mushrooms, washed, trimmed, and soaked for 3−4 hours
2 teaspoons sesame oil
1 large carrot, peeled
10 spring onions
2 eggs, separated into white and yolk, beaten, fried separately, and cut into thin strips
20 gingko nuts
2 tablespoons pine nuts
2 pints (1 litre) rich homemade chicken broth (see p. 69)

Pound the steak lightly with a meat hammer to tenderize. Cut into very thin slices across the grain. Season with salt and pepper.

Dip the slices of steak first in flour, then in beaten egg. Heat some vegetable oil in a frying pan and fry over a medium heat for about 2−3 minutes a side. Drain on kitchen paper, then cut into 1 in (2.5 cm) squares.

Thinly slice the chicken, fish fillets, and liver. Season, and dip each in flour, then beaten egg, and fry in the same manner. Drain on kitchen paper and cut into 1 in (2.5 cm) squares.

In a bowl, mix the ground beef with the spring onion, ginger, soy sauce, and garlic. Form into small balls (about $\frac{1}{2}$ in/12 mm in diameter). Dip first in flour, then in beaten egg and fry in hot oil until crisp. Drain on kitchen paper.

Wash the bean sprouts and take off the little hairlike rootlets, then chop coarsely. Drain the mushrooms, squeeze out excess water. Cut them into neat strips, then fry in sesame oil until tender. Cut the carrot into similar sized thin strips.

To assemble the *shinsollo*, first place the chopped bean sprouts in the bottom of the pot. Next add alternate layers of fried steak, chicken, fish, liver, and meatballs. This should nearly fill the pot. Arrange the top decoratively like colourful spokes, alternating strips of egg white, egg yolk, mushrooms, carrots, and spring onions. Garnish decoratively with gingko nuts and pine nuts.

Before serving, pour boiling stock carefully into the pot, and heat at the table. (*Shinsollo* pots have a central receptacle in which to place burning charcoal: if using, make sure to allow adequate ventilation.) Bring the liquid to the boil and heat the food through before serving direct from the pot.

PASANJOK BEEF AND SPRING ONION KEBABS

파산적

This recipe and the one that follows are both exceedingly simple variations on a theme, yet they are so delicious. They seem to taste better when threaded on to wooden skewers (not metal), and cooked over hot coals. Perhaps it is the taste of charred wood.

$\frac{1}{2}$lb (250 g) sirloin steak
10 spring onions
1 tablespoon soy sauce
$\frac{1}{2}$ tablespoon rice wine or dry sherry
2 teaspoons sesame oil
$\frac{1}{2}$ teaspoon sugar
2 garlic cloves, peeled, crushed, and finely chopped
1 tablespoon toasted sesame seeds
Freshly ground black pepper

Slice the steak into thin strips. Trim the spring onions and cut into similar lengths as the beef strips. Thread the beef and spring onions on to bamboo skewers (run the skewers through one end of the beef and onions, not the middle, so that they dangle down like a curtain). Mix together the soy sauce, wine, sesame oil, sugar, garlic, sesame seeds, and black pepper and pour over the beef and onion skewers. Leave to marinade for 1 hour. Cook over a charcoal fire, or under a grill for about 5–7 minutes a side.

SONGISANJOK BEEF AND MUSHROOM KEBABS

송이산적

Strictly speaking, the mushrooms used in this simple kebab dish should be wild pine mushrooms; but choose large-capped field mushrooms as a most tasty and suitable alternative.

$\frac{1}{2}$lb (250 g) sirloin steak
About 6 large-capped field mushrooms, washed and sliced
1 tablespoon soy sauce
$\frac{1}{2}$ tablespoon rice wine or dry sherry
2 teaspoons sesame oil
$\frac{1}{2}$ teaspoon sugar
2 garlic cloves, peeled, crushed, and finely chopped
1 in (2.5 cm) piece of fresh ginger, peeled, crushed, and finely chopped

1 tablespoon toasted sesame seeds
Freshly ground black pepper

Follow the method for beef and spring onion kebabs above, but substitute the mushrooms for the spring onions.

Journal Notes

Tongdaemun Sijang — Great East Gate Market
Tongdaemun, one of nine gates that originally pierced the Seoul city wall, is a massive and imposing structure, with a double pagoda roof, and a crenellated inner wall serving as a further line of defence. It is a classic example of late Yi dynasty architecture. Today it stands serenely in the middle of a busy intersection, encircled by cacophony and traffic.

We visited Tongdaemun Sijang today, the immense market that is said to be the largest in Korea, possibly in Far East Asia. It is a maze of partly-covered alleys; of vast and tiny stalls; of tall buildings selling virtually everything you could ever possibly need, from silks to blue jeans, pots and pans to delicate inlaid lacquerware, hardware and handicrafts to mountain climbing gear and other sports equipment.

And of course there is food! We wandered through the eating tents, past mountains of well-glazed pigs' heads; pots full of chapchae; *platters of fried fritters,* pindaettok *and* pajon; *stuffed laver rolls; and bubbling cauldrons filled with unidentified treasures. To pass by and admire is to be beckoned to a table, and we enjoyed a fine feast of finger food, together with a few bottles of* OB maekchu.

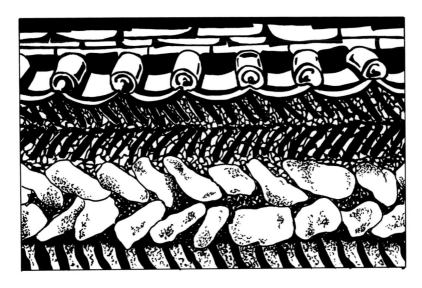

KOREAN POT ROAST

뚝배기

This is a variation of *changjorim* to be eaten not as a condiment, but in large slices *haole*-style. Left-over meat is excellent added to noodle dishes, especially *naengmyon*, or for stir-fry or fried rice dishes.

3–4 lb (1.5–2 kg) piece of rolled rump or sirloin
½ pint (300 ml) soy sauce
1¼ pints (750 ml) water
12 fresh chillies
12 carrots, peeled, and cut into 4 in (10 cm) pieces

Place the meat in a large pot or casserole and add the soy sauce, water, and fresh chillies. Bring to a simmer and cook partially covered for about 2–2½ hours, turning occasionally. Add the carrots about 20 minutes before the end of cooking time.

Allow to cool in the broth. Remove and discard fat. Cut into thin slices and arrange on a platter together with the cooked chillies and carrots. Serve the chilli broth as a sauce.

MEAT FRITTERS

고기전

These meat fritters are so simple and delicious cut up into little squares and eaten hot or cold, together with a saucer of vinegar dipping sauce. Serve them with other *jon*, *namul*, *kimchi*, and rice.

1½ lb (750 g) sirloin steak
Salt
Freshly ground black pepper

4 tablespoons flour
2 eggs, beaten by hand
Vegetable oil for frying

Cut the steak into very thin slices on the slant. Pound lightly with a meat hammer to tenderize and season with salt and pepper.

Heat oil in a large frying pan. Press the steak slices first in flour, then in beaten egg. Fry over medium heat until brown and crispy, about 2–3 minutes; turn and cook on the other side. Drain on kitchen towel, cut into 2 in (5 cm) squares, and arrange on a serving platter. Serve with *chojang* vinegar dipping sauce.

KOREAN 'HAMBURGERS'

완자전

These minced meat patties, spiked with fresh chillies, spring onions, *kimchi*, garlic, and ginger, are actually quite authentic. Halmoni makes the patties the size of a burger; in Korea, they might be made about a quarter of that size, or else broken up into pieces and served in a communal dish. Eaten '*haole* style', with some rice and salad, they make an excellent quick supper.

1 lb (500 g) lean minced beef
3 spring onions, finely chopped
$\frac{1}{2}$ in (12 mm) piece of fresh ginger, peeled, and finely chopped
1 garlic clove, peeled, crushed, and finely chopped
$\frac{1}{2}$ cup *kimchi*, rinsed, and chopped (if available)
1–2 fresh chillies, finely chopped
1 teaspoon sesame oil
1 teaspoon soy sauce
1 tablespoon flour
1 egg to bind

In a large bowl, mix all the ingredients together. Form into small patties. Fry or cook over charcoal, or under a grill. Serve with *chojang* vinegar dipping sauce.

Journal Notes

Two Angry Women
Kim and Michele returned to the hotel room this evening, furious. After enjoying the bathhouses of Paegam, they had been looking forward to relaxing in the saunatang here in the hotel in Chonju. But when they went down-stairs, they were told, 'Men only.'

Absolutely outrageous, I sympathized, as I picked up my sponge bag and padded down for a few hours of peace and relaxation in the hot tub, cold tank, and sauna, followed by maekchu and peanuts served by a beautiful hostess. Afterwards, I returned upstairs to our room and babysat while Kim and Michele went downstairs to the cocktail bar to sulk.

WANJAJON BEEF AND BEAN CURD PATTIES

완자전

A variation of Korean 'hamburgers': equally simple and delicious.

$\frac{1}{2}$ cake bean curd
$\frac{1}{2}$ lb (250 g) lean minced beef
1 teaspoon soy sauce
1 teaspoon sesame oil
2 spring onions, finely chopped
2 garlic cloves, peeled, crushed, and finely chopped
1 tablespoon toasted sesame seeds
Salt
Freshly ground black pepper
Flour
1 egg, beaten
Vegetable oil for frying

Squeeze the excess moisture from the bean curd, crumble, and mix with the minced beef, soy sauce, sesame oil, spring onions, garlic, sesame seeds, salt, and black pepper. Shape into small patties about $1\frac{1}{2}$ in (3.5 cm) in diameter. Press them in flour, then dip in beaten egg. Heat the oil in a frying pan and fry until golden brown on both sides, about 5 minutes each. Drain on kitchen paper and serve with *chojang* vinegar dipping sauce.

Kyerim 'Chicken Forest'

Kyerim is a moody, cool, unspoiled forest on the edge of Kyongju city, not far from the famous burial mounds which dominate the area, their grassy, massive slopes rising above the grey-tiled roofs of the city as grandiose monuments to a splendid past. It is hard today to imagine that this small provincial town of only around a hundred thousand inhabitants was once a sprawling capital ten times that size.

Kyerim is especially important for members of the Kyongju Kim clan, Halmoni's family, for it was here in the first century AD that Sok Talhae was awakened by a rooster announcing the discovery of a baby boy in a gold box, hanging from an elm tree. That baby was named Kim Alchi (Kim means gold), and was to be the first in line of a venerable dynasty which then went on to rule as kings of Silla.

TAKKUI MARINADED BARBECUED CHICKEN

닭구이

Takkui — marinaded barbecued chicken — is one of our all-time favourites, but to be really exceptional, two things are essential: first slash the chicken almost to the bone, and second, marinade the chicken pieces overnight. These savoury chicken pieces always taste best when cooked over hot charcoal.

1 whole chicken, cut into 8 pieces, or 8 chicken thighs

Marinade
3 garlic cloves, peeled, crushed, and finely chopped
1 in (2.5 cm) piece of fresh ginger, peeled, crushed, and finely chopped
4 tablespoons soy sauce
2 tablespoons sesame oil
2 teaspoons toasted sesame seeds
1 tablespoon sugar
Freshly ground black pepper
5 spring onions, sliced

Slash the chicken pieces diagonally almost to the bone in several places, and place in a deep bowl. Mix together the marinade ingredients and pour over the chicken pieces, mixing it in well with the hands. Leave for several hours or overnight, turning and mixing frequently.

Prepare a medium-hot charcoal grill. Raise the grill about 3 in (7.5 cm) from the fire. When ready, place the chicken pieces skin-side down. Be ready to control any flare-ups, and turn frequently, until both sides are crispy brown, and the chicken is cooked right through (about 25–35 minutes in all).

Since chicken usually absorbs less marinade than, say, beef, we like to add a little water to the remaining marinade, then, in a pot, bring it to the boil to make a delicious acccompanying sauce. Place the grilled chicken pieces in a clean bowl, and pour this sauce over them.

TAKSANJOK CHICKEN AND SPRING ONIONS ON SKEWERS

달산적

Taksanjok is another exceedingly simple but delicious food, best cooked over charcoal, or under a hot grill.

1½–2 lb (750 g–1 kg) skinless, boneless chicken thighs
About 20 small spring onions

Marinade
2 garlic cloves, peeled, crushed, and finely chopped
½ in (12 mm) piece of fresh ginger, peeled, crushed, and finely chopped
4 tablespoons soy sauce
1 tablespoon sesame oil
1 tablespoon toasted sesame seeds
1 tablespoon sugar
1 tablespoon vegetable oil

About 15–20 bamboo skewers

Cut the chicken into even pieces, about 3 or 4 from each thigh. Cut the spring onions into pieces roughly equal in length. Thread them alternately on to the wooden skewers, about 3 pieces of chicken and 3 onion lengths to each.

Lay the skewers of chicken and spring onion in a flat dish, mix the marinade ingredients together, and pour it over the skewers. Allow to marinade for 2–3 hours or longer.

Grill over hot charcoal or under a grill, about 5–7 minutes a side or until cooked through.

TAKPOKKUM CHICKEN BRAISED IN SOY SAUCE

달복음

1 whole chicken or 8 chicken thighs
4 tablespoons soy sauce
1 tablespoon sesame oil
3 garlic cloves, peeled, crushed, and finely chopped
1 in (2.5 cm) piece of fresh ginger, peeled, crushed, and finely chopped
2 tablespoons toasted sesame seeds
4 spring onions, chopped
1 tablespoon sugar

Freshly ground black pepper
1 green pepper, seeded and coarsely diced
1 red pepper, seeded and coarsely diced

Cut the chicken up into about 16 small pieces (if using chicken thighs, cut each in two). Mix together the soy sauce, sesame oil, garlic, ginger, sesame seeds, spring onions, sugar, and black pepper. Add to the chicken and allow to marinate for 3—4 hours or overnight.

When ready to cook, remove from the marinade, heat a little oil in a large frying pan, and fry the chicken for 5 minutes, or until brown. Add the reserved marinade plus sufficient water to come halfway up the chicken. Bring to the boil, cover partially, and simmer until the chicken is cooked through, about 30—40 minutes. If there is still a lot of cooking liquid, uncover and boil vigorously to reduce. Add the diced peppers and cook for a further 5 minutes, then serve immediately.

TWAEJIGOGIGUI HOT BARBECUED PORK

돼지갈비구이

This hot barbecued pork is a simple and spicy dish: serve it with lots of rice and a fresh green salad.

6 thin pork steaks or boneless chops
2 tablespoons *kochujang*
2 teaspoons red pepper powder
1 tablespoon soy sauce
1 tablespoon sesame oil
3 garlic cloves, peeled, crushed, and finely chopped
1 in (2.5 cm) piece of fresh ginger, peeled, crushed, and finely chopped
1 tablespoon sugar

Lightly score the pork steaks or chops in a diamond pattern. Mix the remaining ingredients together and spread this paste thinly over the meat. Leave to marinade for 30 minutes.

Prepare a charcoal fire (or else cook under a grill), and cook for 5—7 minutes a side until cooked through.

TWAEJIGALBIGUI BARBECUED SPARE RIBS

돼지고기구이

The same basic *pulgogi* marinade works extremely well on pork spare ribs. The key to cooking ribs really well, that is, charred and crunchy on the outside but succulent and sweet inside, is first to parboil them before marinading and cooking them over charcoal or under a grill. Though the amount of sugar in this recipe may seem excessive, it ensures that the ribs become well glazed.

2 lb (1 kg) pork spare ribs
5 tablespoons soy sauce
2 tablespoons sesame oil
3 tablespoons sugar
4 spring onions, finely chopped
3 garlic cloves, peeled, crushed, and finely chopped
1 in (2.5 cm) piece of fresh ginger, peeled, crushed, and finely chopped
1 tablespoon toasted sesame seeds
Plenty of freshly ground black pepper

Cut the spare ribs into 2½ in (6 cm) pieces, and score deeply in 3 or 4 places on each rib. Place the ribs in a pot, pour on boiling water, and cook for 5 minutes. Drain well, and transfer to a large bowl. Mix together the marinade ingredients, and pour over the ribs. Mix well and leave for a least 2–3 hours, turning occasionally.

Prepare a charcoal grill (or pre-heat a grill). Arrange the ribs on a rack and cook over the hot coals or under the grill for about 10–12 minutes, turning frequently. Have a sprinkler (or water pistol) on hand to damp down any flare-ups from the fire.

TWAEJIGOGIGIMCHIBOKKUM STIR-FRIED PORK AND *KIMCHI*

돼지고기김치복음

This hot and sour stir-fry is really delicious: bracing, warming winter fare. Use slightly old or sour *kimchi*, but make sure to rinse it well first.

1 lb (500 g) boneless pork steaks
1 tablespoon *kochujang*
2 spring onions, finely chopped
1 teaspoon sugar

2 garlic cloves, peeled, crushed, and finely chopped
1 tablespoon toasted sesame seeds
Freshly ground black pepper

About 6−8 oz (175−250 g) *kimchi*
1 onion, peeled and thinly sliced
2 fresh red chillies, seeded and cut into thin strips

1 tablespoon vegetable oil

Cut the pork into thin strips. Mix with the *kochujang*, spring onions, sugar, garlic, sesame seeds, and plenty of black pepper. Rinse the *kimchi* and squeeze dry. Slice into similar-size strips as the pork.

Heat the vegetable oil in a large frying pan and stir-fry the seasoned pork for about 5 minutes. Then add the *kimchi*, sliced onion, and chilli strips. Stir-fry for a further 5 minutes, then add about $\frac{1}{2}$ pint (300 ml) of water, cover and cook for 10 minutes, or until the pork is cooked through. Transfer to a platter and serve with hot steamed rice.

KANJON LIVER FRITTERS

간 전

I confess that I have never been a great fan of liver, but treated in the Korean manner, that is, lightly dredged in flour and beaten egg, then panfried, it is delicious, particularly as part of a platter of different fried foods − *modun jon*.

1 lb (500 g) liver
Water
1 tablespoon vinegar
Salt
Freshly ground black pepper
1 tablespoon flour
1 egg, beaten by hand
Vegetable oil for frying

Trim the liver of any tough membranes. Soak in water with a tablespoon of vinegar added for 1 hour. Remove, pat dry, and cut into thin slices on the slant. Score each slice, then season with salt and pepper. Dredge first in flour, then dip in beaten egg. Heat a little vegetable oil in a frying pan, and fry until golden brown and just crispy, about 3−5 minutes a side. Serve at once.

8
Seafood and Shellfish

Pusan is Korea's second city, a vast, bustling industrial port with a population of over four million. When Halmoni sent my mother and her brother John there from Hawaii to be looked after by their Aunt, my Great Aunt, the city was of vital importance to the Japanese who then occupied the country, for it lies a mere 120 miles (193 kilometres) from Honshu, Japan's main island.

Today, Pusan remains one of the country's largest industrial centres, and also one of its major ports, a centre not only for shipping, but also for the fishing industry. Pusan's Chagalchi Fish Market is undoubtedly the biggest and most outstanding in the country. Situated right down by the main working harbour, it is a vast and slippery pavilion bustling with life and activity from the earliest hours of the morning. Here, the great trawlers of the East Coast, as well as those shallower-draft boats that work the waters off the southern and western shores, land a spectacular and awesome catch. Great octopus, shark and tuna hang from huge iron hooks, while an astonishing array of smaller fry — mackerel, pollock, red snapper, anchovies, sardines, skate, cod, croaker, corvina and much else — are all piled high in plastic trays and tubs of ice. Enormous king crabs wriggle alongside tiny blue crabs while buckets of oysters, mussels, clams, abalone, eel, king prawns, sea cucumbers, sea squirt and mud snails vie for the attention of wholesalers, restaurateurs and individual shoppers.

Considering this remarkable array of the freshest fish available, the dried fish area is equally staggering, for immense quantities of dried and semi-dried mackerel, swordfish, pollock, anchovies and other fish are piled high, or strung up with straw into lines, giving off a heady and salty aroma. Such dried fish is still a basic food for a great majority of the population as is seaweed, piled or hanging from wires like green curtains from the sea.

WHOLE-FRIED FISH KOREAN STYLE
생선튀김

When Halmoni cooks this fish it is really theatrical: the whole floured fish is thrown into a pan of sizzling hot oil so that it crisps up and crackles wildly. Once cooked, she then drains the oil, heats up the fiery chilli sauce in the frying pan, then spreads it over the crispy skin. Finally, it is transferred in all its glory on to a serving platter layered with a bed of cool, freshly-chopped lettuce, and garnished with shredded spring onions and chopped fresh coriander.

1 whole round fish (such as sea bass, red mullet, pollock, or whiting), about 1−1½ lb/500−750 g), cleaned
2 heaped tablespoons flour, seasoned with salt and pepper
Vegetable oil for frying

Sauce
3 garlic cloves, peeled, crushed, and finely chopped
1 in (2.5 cm) piece of fresh ginger, peeled, crushed, and finely chopped
1 tablespoon *kochujang*
2 tablespoons soy sauce
1 tablespoon sesame oil
1 teaspoon Chinese salted black beans, crumbled
½ tablespoon sugar

1 lettuce, washed and finely shredded
2 spring onions, shredded on the diagonal
Handful fresh coriander, finely chopped

Clean the fish and scale if necessary. Dredge in the seasoned flour on both sides and shake off the excess. Heat up a frying pan large enough to hold the whole fish with about 1 inch (2.5 cm) vegetable oil. When the oil is just smoking, add the fish and fry for about 7−10 minutes a side (depending on size) or until cooked through.

In the meantime, mix together the sauce ingredients. When the fish is cooked, remove, and pat dry on kitchen paper. Drain the oil from the frying pan, turn the heat down to low, and add the sauce. Cook, stirring all the while, for 2−3 minutes.

Prepare a serving platter by covering with a bed of shredded lettuce. Transfer the whole fish to the platter. Spread the sauce over the fish, and garnish with spring onions and fresh coriander.

SAENGSONJON FRIED FISH FILLETS

생선전

These easy-to-make fried fish fillets are a good addition to a mixed platter of fried foods — *modun jon* — together with aubergine fritters, fried courgette slices, stuffed chillies, and meat fritters. Equally, they are delicious on their own, with rice, *kimchi*, and *namul*. As always, choose the freshest fish you can find.

1 lb (500 g) white fish fillets (cod or haddock)
1 teaspoon salt
Vegetable oil for frying
2 tablespoons flour
1–2 eggs, beaten by hand

Slice the fish fillets on the slant into thin, even pieces. Sprinkle the fish with a little salt. Heat a little vegetable oil in a frying pan to medium hot. Dredge the fish slices first in flour, then dip in beaten egg. Fry in hot oil for about 3–5 minutes a side or until brown and cooked through. Serve with *chojang* vinegar dipping sauce.

SAENGSONGUI I BARBECUED WHOLE FISH

생선구이

Though Koreans may prefer to eat really fresh fish raw (*saengsonhoe*), we think that nothing can beat fresh fish, marinaded briefly, then grilled over hot coals. The type of fish you use doesn't really matter: just choose whatever is available and really fresh.

1 whole large fish (about 1 lb/500 g), mullet, sea bass, mackerel, or sole, cleaned

3 tablespoons soy sauce
1 tablespoon sesame oil
2 garlic cloves, peeled, crushed, and finely chopped
$\frac{1}{2}$ in (12 mm) piece of fresh ginger, peeled, crushed, and finely chopped
2 spring onions, shredded on the diagonal
1 tablespoon sugar
1 tablespoon toasted sesame seeds
1 teaspoon red pepper powder
Freshly ground black pepper

Clean and scale the fish if necessary. Wash well, then cut 3 or 4 deep diagonal slashes on each side.

Mix all the other ingredients together and pour over the fish, working the mixture well into the slits. Leave for 20–30 minutes.

Meanwhile, prepare a charcoal fire if using (otherwise cook under a grill). When the coals are white hot, place the fish on a rack and cook for about 7–10 minutes each side, or until done, depending on the thickness of the fish. Serve at once.

SAENGSONGUI II SALT-GRILLED WHOLE FISH

생선구 이

Given the abundance of such fine fresh fish throughout Korea, it always surprises me that dried salted and semi-salted fish remains such a favourite basic (the same can be said about the Italians and their love of *baccalà*). In Korea, even fresh fish is often salted for a brief period before being cooked over hot coals. The result may well seem rather too salty for our tastes, but do remember that such fish is really meant to be eaten in small pieces, not as a main course, but more as a pungent and flavourful condiment to accompany large quantities of steamed white rice, *kimchi*, and *namul*. Fresh mackerel lends itself to this treatment particularly well.

1 large whole mackerel (about 1 lb/500 g), cleaned and gutted
3 tablespoons sea salt

Wash the cleaned and gutted fish thoroughly. Score deeply with 3 or 4 slashes on each side. Sprinkle the inside and outside with sea salt and set aside for 30 minutes.

Meanwhile, prepare a hot charcoal fire (or else pre-heat a grill). Wipe the fish with a cloth to remove excess moisture and salt, then place on a rack and grill, about 8–10 minutes a side depending on its size. When cooked, place the fish on a platter and serve accompanied by saucers of *chojang* vinegar dipping sauce.

TOMI-TCHIM STEAMED RED SNAPPER

도 미찜

Tomi-tchim, red snapper stuffed decoratively with meat and strips of vegetables, and cooked in a steamer, is fancy, decorative food from the Yi dynasty palace tradition. But though this dish may seem rather complicated, the visual effect — as well as the flavour — is quite stunning. If red snapper, the favoured Korean fish, is not available, then substitute a really fresh flat fish such as sole.

Korean Ceramics

Graceful wine ewers of double gourd shape glazed a glorious grey-green, the colour of a kingfisher's crest; delicate lobed dishes the shape of chrysanthemum flowers, a grey-slate tint like the sky after rain; petalled wine cups with formal pedestal stands inlaid with slip decorations of flying cranes, willows or peony scrolls; covered bowls decorated with garlands of lotus blossoms and fantastic dragons and phoenixes frolicking among stylized clouds: these are the famous celadons of the Koryo dynasty (tenth to fourteenth centuries), ceramics so finely wrought and decorated that they are rightly considered one of Korea's great cultural achievements.

There is little doubt that the techniques for producing fine celadon ware came to Korea from Sung dynasty China, but the Korean potters of the Koryo period produced pieces which, if not as formal or even as technically perfect as those of their influential neighbour, were far more spontaneous and naturalistic in form and design. Pots, cups, bowls and urns became gourds, melon flowers, bamboo shoots, ducks and geese; the celadon glazes were perfected into as many as sixty unique and identifiable shades; and, as well, a most elaborate process of inlaying designs (known as *sanggam*) by etching out recesses in the leather-hard body then filling them in with white or black slip and smoothing them out into one uniform surface, was perfected.

The fragile art of producing fine ceramic ware is one that has been practised in Korea for centuries. If china and tableware can be viewed as an expression of a nation's character and aesthetic, then the classic stoneware of the Silla period, the elegant and naturalistic forms and delicate celadons of the Koryo, and the later spontaneous *punchong* pottery of the Yi dynasty, all reflect a temperament at once exuberant and self-assured, one which sees a wine cup first of all as a cup from which to drink wine, but none the less beautiful for having to serve that joyous daily role.

1 whole red snapper (about $1-1\frac{1}{2}$ lb/500−750 g) or whole sole

---

$\frac{1}{4}$ lb (125 g) lean ground beef
1 teaspoon sesame oil
1 garlic clove, peeled, crushed, and finely chopped
$\frac{1}{2}$ in (12 mm) piece of fresh ginger, peeled, crushed, and finely chopped
Freshly ground black pepper

$\frac{1}{2}$ cucumber, cut into thin matchsticks
1 small carrot, peeled and cut into thin matchsticks
4 mushrooms, sliced
$\frac{1}{2}$ bunch watercress, cut into 1 in (2.5 cm) pieces
$\frac{1}{2}$ red pepper, seeded and cut into thin strips
2 eggs, separated into white and yolk, beaten, fried, and cut into thin strips
2 spring onions, shredded on the diagonal

Clean the fish and scale if necessary. Wash well then cut 3−4 deep diagonal slashes on one side. Mix the beef with the seasonings, and stuff this mixture into the slits of the fish. Place the stuffed fish on a rack in a large pot or wok and steam for 15−20 minutes.

Remove the fish from the steamer, and carefully arrange the prepared vegetables and egg strips on top of the fish, alternating each ingredient to create an attractive, colourful effect. Return to the steamer and steam for another 5 minutes, or until the fish is cooked through. Transfer to a large platter and serve at once.

SAENGSONHOE RAW FISH WITH RED PEPPER SAUCE AND VINEGAR MUSTARD SAUCE

생선회

The place to buy fish in Pusan may be at the Chagalchi Market, but the place to eat it is at any number of *saengsonhoe-jib* located by the waterfront, here or along Haeundae Beach and other seaside resorts that extend on either side of this great city. In such 'raw fish joints', the fish on offer is displayed in aquariums in the front window. You point to the fish that you would like, the proprietor skilfully nets it, you are taken off to your *ondol* room, where you might first nibble on appetizers like sea cucumber, sea squirt, or sea urchin, and before long, your fish is presented to you, skinned, filleted, sliced, and reassembled on the skeleton. Once you've enjoyed this super-fresh feast, the bones and carcase are whisked away to be made into a quick *maeuntang* — hot fish soup — to finish off the meal.

Almost any fish is suitable for eating raw, provided it is absolutely fresh (even such a fairly strong sea fish as mackerel is delicious raw when straight out of the sea). However, we particularly like delicate flat fish such as small halibut, sole, or plaice. They are easier to fillet than round fish and make a most attractive presentation, reassembled on the skeleton. Otherwise choose a sea bream, red snapper, or any other really fresh fish.

A word of warning: Eating uncooked fish is not without its risks: it really is essential that you know your fishmonger and that you skin and fillet the fresh fish yourself so that you can ensure that you avoid contamination from unwanted surface bacteria. The best way, of course, is to prepare and eat fish that you have just caught yourself.

1 whole flat fish (choose whatever is available and really fresh — halibut, lemon sole, Dover sole, or plaice)
1 Korean radish, finely grated

Red Pepper Sauce
2 tablespoons *kochujang*
1 tablespoon rice or cider vinegar
$\frac{1}{2}$ tablespoon sesame oil
1 garlic clove, peeled, crushed, and finely chopped
$\frac{1}{2}$in (12 mm) piece of fresh ginger, peeled, crushed, and finely chopped
3 spring onions, finely chopped

Vinegar Mustard Sauce
2 tablespoons soy sauce

1 tablespoon rice or cider vinegar
$\frac{1}{2}$–1 tablespoon hot green mustard

Carefully clean the fresh fish, then fillet and skin it. Slice the fillets on the diagonal into thin pieces, then reassemble on the skeleton carcase. Place the finely grated Korean radish on a large platter, and arrange the reassembled fish on this bed.

Mix together the two sauce ingredients in separate bowls. Serve immediately.

After eating, use the bones and carcase to make *maeuntang*.

SAENGSONSANJOK SKEWERED FISH AND BEEF

생선산적

We have always believed that meat and seafood make delicious combinations — witness such classics as Portuguese *amêijoas na cataplana* (pork and clams) or British steak and oyster pudding. These meat and fish skewers are simple but equally successful.

$\frac{1}{4}$ lb (125 g) sirloin steak
1 tablespoon soy sauce
$\frac{1}{2}$ teaspoon sugar
1 teaspoon sesame oil
1 teaspoon toasted sesame seeds
1 spring onion, finely chopped
Freshly ground black pepper

$\frac{1}{2}$ lb (250 g) firm white fish (cod or haddock) fillets, unskinned
Salt
2 teaspoons sesame oil

Cut the beef into strips about 2 in (5 cm) long and $\frac{1}{4}$ in (6 mm) wide. Mix the soy sauce, sugar, sesame oil, sesame seeds, spring onion, and black pepper together and add to the beef. Set aside to marinade for 30 minutes.

Cut the fish into similar-sized strips, leaving the skin attached. Sprinkle with salt to taste and sesame oil.

Thread the meat and fish alternately on to bamboo skewers and cook over a hot charcoal fire (or under a grill) for about 3–5 minutes a side (do not overcook or the fish will disintegrate).

Journal Notes

Haeundae Beach
Arrived today at Haeundae Beach, a long, fine crescent of sand on the northeast side of Pusan.

It is rather unseasonable — but the shellfish gatherers and fisherfolk are out wading amongst the rocks at low tide, their baggy paji *trousers gathered up to their waists as they dig and search for abalone, clams, sea urchins and other such creatures. Further round, by the small fishing harbour, are a number of colourful small tents. There, the fisherwomen sit in front of basins full of wriggling creatures. They are quite insistent, these fisherwomen, their heads wrapped in towels and visors, the glint of a gold capped tooth catching your eye as they beckon and smile.*

They urge you to come into a tent, your own private ondol *tent — shoes off please — which looks out across the wide bay to where the mountains of Pusan come down to the sea. A few quick swipes with a knife and that live octopus is dispatched and placed in front of you. Raw sea cucumber is another favourite similarly dealt with: though this valued speciality may seem rather slimy and unappetizing, when chopped up and eaten raw, the taste is not at all strong, but sea-fresh and bitter.* Mongge *— sea squirt — is a weird, warty, orange thing, another such food that looks far worse than it tastes: it is particularly favoured as a food to whet the appetite. And of course, sea urchin, cut in half, the orange middle scooped out with a spoon or chopstick, is another popular delicacy.*

DEEP-FRIED RED MULLET
홍어구이

Red mullet is one of our favourite fish, both pretty to look at and delicious to eat.

1 large red mullet or 2−4 small ones
Salt
Freshly ground black pepper
Flour for dredging
Vegetable oil for deep-frying

3 tablespoons soy sauce
1 tablespoon sesame oil
1 in (2.5 cm) piece of fresh ginger, peeled, and cut into matchstick slivers
2 teaspoons sugar
2 teaspoons toasted sesame seeds

**1 fresh green or red chilli, seeded and finely chopped
2 spring onions, shredded on the diagonal**

Clean and scale the fish. Make 3 diagonal slashes on each side. Season with salt and pepper, and dredge in flour. Heat sufficient oil until just smoking and fry the fish until crisp and cooked through, probably about 7−10 minutes, depending on the size of the fish. Drain on kitchen paper. Arrange the fried fish on a platter.

Meanwhile, mix the remaining ingredients (except the spring onions) together in a pan and bring to the boil. Pour this sauce over the fish and garnish with shredded spring onions.

PUGOGUI DRIED POLLOCK WITH CHILLI SAUCE

북 어구 이

Pugo − dried pollock − is an extremely popular Korean staple, and is always available from Korean groceries. Though rather forbidding to look at, it is nonetheless an authentic taste of the land. This is how Halmoni prepares it: chewy, sweet, and hot.

2 split dried pollock

**1 tablespoon *kochujang*
1 garlic clove, peeled, crushed, and finely chopped
$\frac{1}{2}$in (12 mm) piece of fresh ginger, peeled, crushed, and finely chopped
2 teaspoons sesame oil
2 teaspoons toasted sesame seeds
2 teaspoons sugar
2 spring onions, finely chopped**

Lay the split dried pollock in a flat dish, and cover with water. Leave to soak only for about 1 hour, until soft and plump. Drain, and squeeze out excess water. Cut the fish into 2 in (5 cm) pieces.

Mix together the *kochujang*, garlic, ginger, sesame oil, sesame seeds, sugar, and spring onions. Spread this chilli paste over the fish slices, and set aside for 30 minutes to steep.

Pre-heat a grill, and cook the fish slices, about 5 minutes a side or until cooked through (they will remain rather tough and chewy).

KE-TCHIM STEAMED STUFFED CRAB

게 찜

Ke-tchim is a delicious way to dress and prepare fresh crab. We first sampled this at the Yong Soo San, a fine *yangban-jib* located behind Kyongbok Palace in Seoul. At the Yong Soo San, uncoventionally, the foods are served one by one in a slow and relaxed procession.

1 large fresh-cooked crab
$\frac{1}{4}$ cake bean curd
2 oz (50 g) bean sprouts
2 spring onions, shredded on the diagonal
1 garlic clove, peeled, crushed, and finely chopped
$\frac{1}{2}$ in (12 mm) piece of fresh ginger, peeled, crushed, and finely chopped
1 teaspoon sesame oil
Salt
Freshly ground black pepper
1 tablespoon flour
1 egg, beaten
1 small lettuce, shredded

Prise open the shell of the crab. Discard the stomach bag, the feathery gills, and other innards. Remove all the flesh from the crab body, and mix together the white and dark meat. Remove the legs and claws, crack, and remove the meat. Add this to the rest. Scrub the crab shell and set aside.

Wrap the bean curd in a cloth and squeeze out excess moisture, then crumble it finely. Blanch the bean sprouts briefly, drain and squeeze out excess moisture, then chop finely. Combine the crab meat with the bean curd, bean sprouts, spring onions, garlic, sesame oil, salt, and pepper. Mix well then restuff into the washed crab shell. Sprinkle the flour on the top, and brush with beaten egg. Place in a steamer and steam for about 15 minutes. Serve on a bed of shredded lettuce.

HAEMULJONGOL SEAFOOD CHONGOL

해물 전골

Chongol is the popular method of cooking any number of ingredients — meat, seafood, and vegetables — in broth at the table:
as such it is not only a delicious method of preparation, it is also
particularly suitable for a festive or special occasion. Choose any
variety of seafood for this version, ensuring, as always, that it is as
fresh as possible.

2 pints (1 litre) small clams or cockles in the shell
1 lb (500 g) squid
1 lb (500 g) white fish fillets (cod, turbot, sea bream)
About 12 Pacific prawns (or giant prawns)
1 bunch watercress or $\frac{1}{2}$ lb (250 g) spinach, cut into 2 in (5 cm)
pieces
2 cakes bean curd, diced
6 spring onions, cut into 2 in (5 cm) pieces
2–3 fresh red or green chillies, seeded and thinly sliced
1 onion, peeled and sliced
2 in (5 cm) piece of fresh ginger, peeled and sliced
$1\frac{1}{4}$ pints (750 ml) fish stock or broth
Salt
Freshly ground black pepper

Clean the clams or cockles, discarding any that do not close when
sharply tapped. Place in a basin or bucket of salt water overnight
to expel sand or grit, rinsing from time to time.

Clean the squid thoroughly, and remove the innards and
'plastic' spine. Cut the tentacles into 2 in (5 cm) pieces, and the
body into rings. Slice the fish fillets into 2 in (5 cm) pieces. Clean
the prawns, and de-vein if necessary.

It may be necessary to cook the *chongol* in 2 or more batches. If
so, divide all the ingredients accordingly, and add the first batch
to a large deep pan or wok (preferably one which can be cooked
over a burner at the table).

Add sufficient fish stock or broth, cover, and cook briskly for
about 10–12 minutes, until the clams have opened (discard any
that haven't), and the fish, squid and prawns have adequately
cooked. Season with salt and black pepper, and serve hot immediately from the pot.

PAEJUJON PAN-FRIED SCALLOPS

패주 전

Sweet, fresh scallops, dredged lightly in flour and beaten egg, then quickly fried are always a favourite.

1 lb (500 g) scallops
Salt
Freshly ground black pepper
1 egg, beaten by hand
1 spring onion, finely chopped
2 tablespoons flour
Vegetable oil for frying

Remove the tough membranes from the scallops and slice them in half or in thirds if they are large. Lightly score them around the edges and season with salt and pepper. Mix the beaten egg with the spring onion. Roll the scallops first in flour, then in the egg mixture. Heat a frying pan with vegetable oil and fry until golden-brown, about 3–5 minutes a side. Drain on kitchen paper and serve hot with *chojang* vinegar dipping sauce.

PAEJUSANJOK SKEWERED SCALLOPS

패주 산적

12–16 large scallops
1 red pepper, seeded and cut into 1 in (2.5 cm) squares
1 green pepper, seeded and cut into 1 in (2.5 cm) squares

2 tablespoons soy sauce
1 tablespoon sesame oil
1 tablespoon rice vinegar
1 tablespoon toasted sesame seeds
1 garlic clove, peeled, crushed, and finely chopped
1 teaspoon red pepper powder
$\frac{1}{2}$ in (12 mm) piece of fresh ginger, peeled, crushed, and finely chopped
Freshly ground black pepper

Remove the tough membranes from the scallops and slice in half or in thirds if large. Lightly score around the edges to prevent them from shrinking when grilled. Thread the scallops and red and green peppers alternately on to bamboo skewers.

Mix together the soy sauce, sesame oil, vinegar, toasted sesame seeds, garlic, red pepper powder, ginger, and black pepper, and pour this mixture over the skewered scallops and peppers. Leave for 30 minutes, turning frequently.

Cook either over a medium-hot charcoal fire or under a grill for about 3–5 minutes a side or until cooked through. Do not overcook or the scallops will be tough and dry.

Journal Notes

Driving in Pusan

Driving in Korea is generally pretty insane, but driving in Pusan is virtually suicidal. I've driven in Rome, Mexico City and central Manhattan; we've survived Athens, rush-hour Los Angeles freeways, and – only a few days earlier – the traffic and chaos of Seoul city centre. But believe me, nothing is as crazy as Pusan! There are intersections where eight lanes converge with no traffic lights or indication of right of way whatsoever. It is a case of the survival of the fittest and you have to muscle in not timidly but at high speed and with your hand constantly on the horn. The taxi drivers are the worst of a bad lot: they will pass you on the right, they will pass you on the left, they will zoom by on the hard shoulder or even climb up on the pavement; they stop suddenly to pick up an additional fare (even though they already have people in the vehicle), pull out just as quickly and with no heed to other traffic, and perform the most outrageous U-turns.

Country roads are hardly any better. Passing at high speed takes place around blind corners or at the tops of hills. Oncoming buses often pull out as you are approaching so that you actually have to brake to a complete halt – horn blaring, fist waving – or suffer a head-on collision. The roads are littered with those vehicles that did not stop. This really is no exaggeration: the accident rate is reportedly one of the highest in the world!

When we returned to England, I rented a car at Heathrow for the drive back down to Devon. It was a beautiful spring day and England seemed greener and more lush than almost anywhere on earth. We were anxious to get home after the long journey. But when a car appeared for a moment as if it was going to pull out in front of me, I took no chances, and broke the peace of the English countryside with a long and sharp blast on my horn, in the style of a Pusan taxi. The startled driver gave me a withering look when I passed, reminding me that here such behaviour behind the wheel is simply 'not on'.

SAEUTCHIM STEAMED STUFFED PACIFIC PRAWNS

새우찜

This recipe calls for rather finicky preparation, but the results are well worth the effort. Choose nice large prawns for a really delicious and attractive dish.

12 large Pacific prawns, uncooked in the shell
1 small carrot, peeled and very finely diced
2 spring onions, very finely chopped
1 egg, beaten
1 teaspoon sesame oil
Salt
Freshly ground black pepper

Remove the heads from the Pacific prawns and set aside. Very carefully slit the shells along the back, and remove the meat. Wash the empty shells and set aside.

Remove the black vein from the prawns, then finely chop them. Mix the chopped prawn meat with the diced carrot, spring onions, beaten egg, and sesame oil. Season with salt and pepper. Stuff this mixture back into the shells carefully. Place in a steamer and steam for 10 minutes. Remove from the steamer and arrange carefully on a platter, replacing the heads of the prawns for decoration.

NAKCHIBOKKUM STIR-FRIED BABY OCTOPUS

낙지볶음

Nakchibokkum is a classic, the sort of spicy, fiery, flavourful nibble that is particularly popular in drinking houses; a food, as we say, that promotes a healthy thirst. If you can't get tender and sweet baby octopus, then substitute squid or cuttlefish.

1 lb (500 g) baby octopus (or substitute squid or cuttlefish)
1 tablespoon vegetable oil
2 garlic cloves, peeled, crushed, and finely chopped
1 carrot, peeled and cut into diagonal slices
1 onion, peeled and sliced lengthwise
1 tablespoon *kochujang*
1–2 tablespoons red pepper powder
2 tablespoons soy sauce
2 spring onions, sliced on the diagonal

2 fresh red or green chillies, seeded and sliced on the diagonal
A little water, if necessary
1 tablespoon toasted sesame seeds

Clean the octopus (or squid or cuttlefish) thoroughly, removing the innards, and cut the tentacles into 2 in (5 cm) lengths, and the body into rings.

Heat the oil in a frying pan or wok and stir-fry the garlic, carrot, and onion for 2−3 minutes. Add the octopus (or squid or cuttlefish) pieces and stir-fry for another 2−3 minutes. Add the *kochujang*, red pepper powder, soy sauce, spring onions, and chillies. Mix well and stir-fry for another 3−5 minutes, then reduce the heat, adding a little water if necessary, and cook until tender (about a further 15 minutes). Transfer to a serving platter, garnish with sesame seeds, and serve at once.

SAEUTWIGIM DEEP-FRIED PACIFIC PRAWNS

새우튀김

12 Pacific prawns or giant prawns, uncooked in the shell
Salt
Freshly ground black pepper
1 egg
About 3 oz (75 g) flour
2 teaspoons black sesame seeds
3−6 tablespoons cold water
Vegetable oil for deep frying

Shell the giant prawns, but leave the tail intact. Remove the black vein and season with salt and pepper.

Mix together the egg, flour, sesame seeds, and sufficient cold water to make a thinnish light batter. Make sure not to overmix — it doesn't really matter if there are a few lumps.

Heat the oil for deep-frying until just smoking. Dip the prawns into the batter, shake off any excess, and fry in the hot oil until crisp and brown (about 3−4 minutes). Drain on kitchen paper and serve immediately with *chojang* vinegar dipping sauce.

9
Vegetables, Bean Curd and Egg Dishes

A visit to any market in Korea demonstrates the importance of vegetables in the daily diet: great mountains of Korean cabbage; giant radishes and turnips in a profusion of sizes and shapes; bundles of bright carrots tied together by their vivid green tops; red and green chillies, pointing erect to the sky; piles of small, fresh ginseng rootlets; long, thin, shiny aubergines; large green courgettes; sweet potato stems and garlic stems tied up in stooks; mustard greens, garland chrysanthemum, spinach, and watercress; wild herbs and roots like *kosari*, *toraji*, *todok*, *chui*; and of course mountains of spring onions, garlic, and root ginger.

Kimchi and *namuls* have been covered in a previous chapter, but such is the range of other cooked vegetable dishes that they deserve a chapter of their own. For vegetables are not merely treated as side dishes or accompaniments, but may hold the same importance as cooked meat or fish dishes. Often meat and/or seafood is mixed with vegetables, even when the latter is the primary ingredient. What is important, as always, is to achieve harmony and balance — of savoury foods with bland; vivid, crisp, steamed foods with lightly fried ones; or fresh, crunchy vegetables with salted or preserved foods.

SANGCHUSSAMJANG LETTUCE BUNDLES WITH BEEF AND CHILLI SAUCE

상추 쌈장

Raw leaf vegetables such as soft lettuce, sesame leaves, or *ssukka* (garland chrysanthemum) are much enjoyed eaten simply as an accompaniment to *pulgogi* and *kalbi*. The method is to take a vegetable leaf, add a spoonful of rice, a piece of grilled meat, and a dollop of *kochujang*, roll the whole thing up into a bundle and pop it into your mouth.

Lettuce leaves served with this delicious hot-and-sweet beef sauce, together with a steaming bowl of rice, however, are virtually a meal in themselves.

The best lettuce to use is the one that you pick straight from your own garden; alternatively, choose a soft lettuce such as red leaf or round lettuce.

---

1 head soft lettuce (red leaf or round)

Sauce
1 tablespoon sesame oil
$\frac{1}{4}$ lb (125 g) lean minced beef (or sirloin steak, very finely chopped)
2 garlic cloves, peeled, crushed, and finely chopped
$\frac{1}{2}$ in (12 mm) piece of fresh ginger, peeled, crushed, and finely chopped
1 tablespoon sesame oil
2 tablespoons rice wine or sherry
2 heaped tablespoons *kochujang*
1 heaped tablespoon sugar
2 spring onions, shredded on the diagonal

Steamed white rice

Arrange the cleaned lettuce leaves on a plate. To make the sauce, add the sesame oil to a pan, and lightly fry the minced beef or steak. Drain off excess fat if necessary. Add all the remaining ingredients (except half the spring onions) and cook over a low flame for about 10 minutes.

Spoon the sauce into a bowl, garnish with the remaining spring onions, and serve hot or cold.

To eat, take a lettuce leaf, add a spoonful of hot rice, then a spoonful of the sauce, roll up into a bundle, and eat with the fingers.

Store any remaining sauce in a screwtop bottle in the refrigerator. It is delicious cold.

KOCHUJON STUFFED CHILLI PEPPERS

고추전

Dredging vegetables, meat, or fish first in flour and egg, then frying them, is a characteristic Korean cooking method known as *jon*. These stuffed chilli peppers are much loved. Remember: when making *jon* it is essential to use the freshest eggs to get a really bright and attractive yellow colour.

About 15–20 large chilli peppers

$\frac{1}{2}$ lb (250 g) lean minced beef (or sirloin steak, very finely chopped)
3 spring onions, finely chopped
1 garlic clove, peeled, crushed, and finely chopped
$\frac{1}{2}$ in (12 mm) piece of fresh ginger, peeled, crushed, and finely chopped
$\frac{1}{2}$ tablespoon soy sauce
2 teaspoons toasted sesame seeds
Freshly ground black pepper

---

2 tablespoons flour
1 large egg, beaten by hand
Vegetable oil for frying

Wash the chilli peppers, cut in half lengthwise and remove the seeds. Mix all the stuffing ingredients together and fill the pepper halves.

Put the flour on one plate and the beaten egg on another. Heat a frying pan with vegetable oil for frying. Pat the stuffed peppers first in the flour, then in the beaten egg. Fry in the hot oil for about 4–5 minutes each side, or until done. Drain on kitchen paper. Serve with *chojang* vinegar dipping sauce.

KAJIJON I AUBERGINE FRITTERS

가지전

Jon are good party or entertaining dishes, says Halmoni. Make up platters with a variety of different kinds to pass around: meat, fish, aubergine, courgettes, stuffed peppers, the more the better. Korean aubergines are long and very thin; therefore, choose the smallest, thinnest that you can find, not big fat round ones.

4 long, thin aubergines
2 tablespoons salt
3 tablespoons flour

1 or 2 eggs, beaten by hand
Vegetable oil for frying

Slice the aubergines on the diagonal into thin slices. Soak in water for 30 minutes. Before cooking, add 2 tablespoons of salt to the water and soak for a further 5 minutes. Drain and pat dry.

Heat vegetable oil in a large frying pan to medium-hot. Dredge the aubergine slices first in flour, then dip in beaten egg. Fry in the hot oil, about 5−7 minutes a side, or until brown and cooked through. Drain on kitchen paper and arrange on a platter in overlapping slices. Serve with *chojang* vinegar dipping sauce.

Journal Notes

Kyongju City Impressions

A fine day today, spent exploring modern Kyongju. First a visit to the city market, a sprawling covered maze that spills out on to pavements where women sit, heads wrapped in towels, selling piles of small fresh ginseng rootlets, mountains of immense Korean cabbage and turnips, fresh chillies, brown-skinned Korean pears, household ironware and clothing. Inside the maze, under waving cloth awnings, there are incredible displays of seafood — large slabs of huge sea fish, tubs of crawling crabs, tanks of squirming live eels and frothy, milky elvers; strung up ropes of salted and slightly salted fish; immense piles of seaweed and kelp; plastic tubs of briny and red pepper-tinged kimchi.

There are stalls selling hanbok, *traditional Korean costume. I bargained fiercely for a costume of maroon* paji *(baggy trousers gathered at the ankles), and a* chogori, *a short vest clasped together with an amber button. (Bargain struck, the stall-holder threw in a motley, fur-lined waistcoat for baby Guy.)*

Then we wandered through the little back alleys of Kyongju, peering here and there into courtyards, glimpsing ondol-heated houses with wavy grey-tiled roofs, paper and lattice-screened doors and windows, and, of course, the ever-present* jang *terrace — a clutch of immense earthenware crocks set beside each dwelling.*

Modern Kyongju is located on the site of the former Silla capital of Kumsong, 'the golden city', which, at its peak of prosperity in the seventh century AD, was one of the great cities of the world with a population that reached over one million. The treasures found in the great burial tombs of Kyongju attest to the high degree of sophistication of the Silla era: the amazing gold crowns and girdles, with their jade 'embryos' and other decorations are vivid demonstrations of the wealth and splendour that was Silla; and the painting of the so-called 'heavenly horse', a magnificent lively depiction of a flying horse painted on a bark horse mudguard, is a further example not only of the high degree of artistry, but also of the enduring vivacity and spirit of the Koreans.

KAJIJON II FRIED STUFFED AUBERGINE

가지전

A rather more elaborate variation: aubergine stuffed with beef and bean curd, dipped in flour and egg, and pan-fried.

**1 medium aubergine
2 tablespoons salt**

**½ cake bean curd
¼ lb (125 g) lean minced beef (or sirloin steak, finely chopped)
2 tablespoons soy sauce
1 spring onion, finely chopped
1 garlic clove, peeled, crushed, and finely chopped
1 tablespoon toasted sesame seeds
Freshly ground black pepper**

**2 tablespoons flour
1 egg, beaten by hand
Vegetable oil for frying**

Slice the aubergines on the diagonal into ½ in (12 mm) slices. Soak in water for 30 minutes. Then, before cooking, add 2 tablespoons salt to the water and soak for a further 5 minutes. Drain and pat dry.

Wrap the bean curd in a cloth and squeeze out excess moisture. Crumble finely, then mix it together with the beef, soy sauce, spring onion, garlic, sesame seeds, and pepper.

Dip the aubergine slices in flour, then spread a spoonful of the meat and bean curd mixture in the centre of each slice. Dip in flour again, then press into beaten egg.

Heat vegetable oil in a large frying pan to medium hot. Fry the aubergine slices in the hot oil for about 5–7 minutes a side until cooked through and golden brown. Drain on kitchen paper and arrange on a platter. Serve with *chojang* vinegar dipping sauce.

HOBAKJON FRIED COURGETTE SLICES

호박전

The key to making really good *jon*, says Halmoni, is to end up with something that is really juicy inside yet crispy brown on the outside. Like all good frying methods, it is a matter of 'surprising' that which you are cooking by placing it in oil that is just hot enough to seal it immediately, yet not so hot that it burns the outside before the inside is cooked. For these fried courgette slices, make sure that you don't overcook them — they must remain crisp and juicy or they are no good.

1 lb (500 g) courgettes (choose medium to large ones)
2 tablespoons salt
2 tablespoons flour
1 or 2 eggs, beaten by hand
Vegetable oil for frying

Slice the courgettes on the diagonal into $\frac{1}{4}$ in (6 mm) slices. Just before they are ready to cook, add 2 tablespoons of salt to a bowl of water and soak for 5 minutes only. Drain and pat dry.

Heat some vegetable oil in a large frying pan to medium hot. Dredge the courgette slices individually first in flour, then dip in beaten egg.

Fry in the hot oil for about 3–4 minutes a side, until brown, but still crisp on the inside. Drain on kitchen paper and arrange on a platter in overlapping slices. Serve with *chojang* vinegar dipping sauce.

HOBAKMUCHIM COURGETTES WITH BEEF

호박무침

1 lb (500 g) courgettes
1 teaspoon salt
$\frac{1}{4}$ lb (125 g) lean minced beef
1 tablespoon soy sauce
1 teaspoon sesame oil
1 spring onion, finely chopped
1 garlic clove, peeled, crushed, and finely chopped
1 teaspoon toasted sesame seeds
Freshly ground black pepper
Vegetable oil for frying

Slice the courgettes into $\frac{1}{4}$ in (6 mm) slices. Sprinkle with salt and set aside for 5–10 minutes. Rinse and drain.

Mix the minced beef together with the other seasonings. Sauté in a little oil until brown.

Add the courgettes and sauté for another 2–3 minutes only. Serve warm or chilled.

COURGETTE FRITTERS

호박전

When my mother once made a big platter of these courgette fritters she set aside a batch especially made without chillies for my then two-year-old niece, Emma. Emma loves the fritters — as we all do — and was enjoying them with great gusto, until she ate by mistake one of the chilli fritters. Her little face screwed up in pain, then she cried and cried. Ice cubes were no help — nothing — until her grandmother gave her some orange wedges to suck. So take note: the chillies in this recipe are optional.

1 lb (500 g) courgettes
1 tablespoon salt
2–3 fresh chillies, chopped, or to taste
2 tablespoons fresh coriander, chopped
Salt
Freshly ground black pepper

---

2 eggs, beaten by hand
4 tablespoons flour
1 tablespoon milk
$\frac{1}{2}$ teaspoon baking powder

Vegetable oil for frying

Slice the courgettes lengthwise into quarters, then dice into small cubes. Place in a bowl together with 1 tablespoon of salt. Cover with water and leave for 5 minutes. Rinse well, and drain.

Mix the batter ingredients together in a large bowl, and add the drained courgette cubes, chillies (if using), coriander, and salt and pepper to taste.

Heat some vegetable oil in a frying pan. Add large spoonfuls of the vegetable batter, and fry until cooked through and brown, about 5 minutes each side. Drain on kitchen paper and serve with *chojang* vinegar dipping sauce.

Korean Costume

There is a picture of Halmoni taken almost the moment she arrived in Honolulu: it depicts a small woman with black hair parted in the middle and tied tightly behind in a bun; she is wearing a (slightly wrinkled) dark silk *chima*, the traditional high-waisted Korean skirt, and a light-coloured *chogori*, the long-sleeved waist-jacket tied at the breast with a long wide ribbon. She gazes directly into the camera, brave, forthright, determined.

Even today in Korea, although Western clothing may be worn by many middle-class people in Seoul and elsewhere, the tra-ditional *chima-chogori* is still worn proudly throughout the country, and not just by older women. Indeed whenever a Korean woman really wants to look special, it is this uniquely elegant − some-times breathtakingly beautiful − traditional costume that she dons.

On the whole, though, only older men wear the male equivalent *paji-chogori*, baggy trousers (*paji*) gathered at the ankles, together with a similar short jacket, clasped usually with an amber or bone button.

During times of mourning, coarse, off-white hemp garments and sandals are worn. Clothing made from *ramie* − cool, gauzy, lightweight − is popular in country districts or to wear around the home. With time, it becomes soft and extremely comfortable; more delicate than linen, cooler than cotton, *ramie* could become the next 'designer' material.

YANGPAJON FRIED ONION SLICES

양파전

The hotter the climate, the sweeter the onions. Choose large Spanish onions for this simple fritter, the sweeter the better.

2 large Spanish onions, peeled
2 tablespoons flour
1 egg, beaten by hand
Vegetable oil for frying

Cut the onions into $\frac{1}{4}$in (6 mm) slices. Be careful not to separate the layers of onion. Heat some vegetable oil in a large frying pan to medium hot. Dredge the onion slices first in flour, then dip in beaten egg. Fry in the hot oil for about 3−5 minutes a side until golden brown. Drain on kitchen paper and arrange on a platter in overlapping slices. Serve with *chojang* vinegar dipping sauce.

KOGUMAJON FRIED SWEET POTATOES

고구마전

Sweet potatoes are another typical and favourite Korean vegetable, prepared again as a flour-and-egg fritter, or else candied with other vegetables.

2 medium sweet potatoes
Salt
2 tablespoons flour
1 egg, beaten by hand
Vegetable oil for frying

Peel the sweet potatoes and slice on the diagonal into $\frac{1}{4}$in (6 mm) slices. Place in a pot of boiling salted water and par-boil for 5—7 minutes. Remove, drain, and pat dry.

Heat some vegetable oil in a large frying pan to medium hot. Dredge the par-boiled sweet potato slices first in flour, then dip in beaten egg. Fry in hot oil for about 5 minutes a side until brown and cooked through. Drain on kitchen paper and arrange on a platter in overlapping slices. Serve with *chojang* vinegar dipping sauce.

YACHAEJORIM CANDIED VEGETABLES

야채조림

Soy-glazed vegetables, sweet and savoury, are an unusual side dish as part of a Korean banquet.

2 carrots, peeled and diced
1 Korean radish, peeled and diced
1 sweet potato, peeled and diced
2 in (5 cm) piece of fresh ginger, peeled and sliced
$\frac{1}{2}$ tablespoon salt
6 tablespoons water
4 oz (125 g) sugar
6 tablespoons soy sauce

Prepare all the vegetables. Add the salt to the water and bring to the boil. Add the diced vegetables and boil for 5 minutes. Add the sugar and soy sauce, lower the heat, partially cover and cook for 15 minutes, stirring from time to time to ensure that the vegetables are evenly glazed and the syrup is absorbed.

Cultivation and Culinary Uses of Korean Ginseng

There is no sight more symbolic of Korea than the strange anthropomorphic ginseng root, trapped within its large bell jar. Ginseng, or *insam* as it is known here, was originally found only in the wilds of remote forests; today it is cultivated in Korea, as well as in parts of China, Japan and the Soviet Union. But it is widely accepted that Korean red ginseng is the finest available.

To process red ginseng, selected, specially cultivated roots are washed by hand, then steamed carefully over a fire, causing their delicate white skin to colour a deep shade of red, before being dry-cured for further lengthy periods. White ginseng, less expensive and more widely available in Korea itself, is dried in wooden racks, or can be eaten fresh.

It should be noted that the Koreans hardly distinguish between plants and herbs as food or medicine: both serve the purpose of promoting good health and maintaining the harmony of forces and energies within the body. Therefore, in Korea, ginseng, a noted source of potent *yang* (male) energy, is widely consumed in a variety of ways. *Samgyae tang-jib* restaurants specialize in serving steamed chicken stuffed with white ginseng, glutinous rice, and jujubes; this dish is regarded as a powerful restorative. Slices of ginseng may be added to any number of cooked dishes. Grandfathers purchase whole roots which they then age in their favourite bottle of liquor. Small, fresh ginseng rootlets are munched raw like carrot sticks, or dipped in honey — a delicious snack. Pieces of dried ginseng are simply chewed like candy or they are boiled to make a quite superb, distinctive and earthy drink, *insam cha*.

KAMJABUCHIM POTATO PANCAKES

감자부침

3 medium potatoes
2 spring onions, finely chopped
2 chillies, seeded and finely chopped
2 tablespoons *kimchi*, rinsed and finely chopped (if available)
1 teaspoon salt
2 tablespoons flour
1 egg, beaten by hand

Vegetable oil for frying

Peel the potatoes and grate. Squeeze out excess moisture then drain. Mix together with the chopped spring onions, chillies, *kimchi* (if using), salt, flour, and egg to form a thick batter.

Heat the vegetable oil in a large frying pan to medium hot. Fry spoonfuls of the mixture in hot oil for about 5—7 minutes a side until brown and cooked through. Drain on kitchen paper and arrange on a platter. Serve with *chojang* vinegar dipping sauce.

BROCCOLI FRITTERS

야채전

1 lb (500 g) broccoli
2 fresh chillies, seeded and chopped
3 tablespoons fresh coriander, chopped
Salt
Freshly ground black pepper

3 eggs, beaten
5 tablespoons flour
1 tablespoon milk
Vegetable oil for frying

Peel the stalks of the broccoli, and discard any tough stems. Slice the stems diagonally into rings; slice the flowers. Mix together the batter ingredients in a large bowl, and add the broccoli, chillies, chopped coriander, and salt and pepper to taste. Mix well.

Heat some vegetable oil in a hot frying pan. Make fritters by adding large spoonfuls of the vegetable batter to the frying pan. Press down with a spatula to flatten and fry until brown, about 3—5 minutes a side. Drain on kitchen paper and serve with *chojang* vinegar dipping sauce.

POSOTJON FRIED STUFFED MUSHROOMS

버섯전

For these stuffed mushrooms, choose large-capped field mushrooms, not small cultivated ones.

8−10 large field mushrooms
$\frac{1}{4}$lb (125 g) lean minced beef (or sirloin steak, finely chopped)
2 tablespoons soy sauce
1 spring onion, finely chopped
1 garlic clove, peeled, crushed, and finely chopped
1 tablespoon toasted sesame seeds
Freshly ground black pepper

2 tablespoons flour
1 egg, beaten by hand
Vegetable oil for frying

Wash the mushrooms and remove the stems. Chop the stems finely. Mix the beef together with the chopped mushroom stems, soy sauce, spring onion, garlic, sesame seeds, and black pepper. Place a spoonful of this mixture in each mushroom cap.

Heat some vegetable oil in a large frying pan to medium hot. Roll the prepared mushrooms first in flour, then dip in beaten egg. Fry in the hot oil, about 5 minutes a side until golden brown on both sides. Drain on kitchen paper and arrange on a platter. Serve with *chojang* vinegar dipping sauce.

Vegetarian Temple Cuisine

When the Yi dynasty superseded the Koryo dynasty in 1392, stern Confucianist thought and codes of behaviour gradually came to replace Buddhism, which had previously enjoyed great prestige and influence in royal and government circles. Buddhists were persecuted and monasteries were ousted from cities and moved to remote mountain outposts. Yet such was the enduring nature of this dominant religion that even today over seven thousand temples remain, dotted throughout the peninsula.

Of course, the monks had always lived fairly austere lives of self-denial, but in the mountains they found that they could forage for their meals, and thus a unique vegetarian temple cuisine developed based on the use of edible wild plants, roots, and mountain herbs.

In central Seoul, a former Buddhist monk, Kim Yon Shik, has opened a restaurant, 'Sanchon' ('Mountain Village Restaurant'), located in Insa-dong, where authentic temple cuisine can be sampled. An entire meal of wild mountain herbs may hardly sound like substantial fare, but the eleven- or thirteen-course meals served at low, comfortable tables in hand-crafted gingko bowls and plates are really quite outstanding, consisting of foods such as acorn curd dressed with wild leeks, *kochujang*, and toasted sesame seeds; wild sesame gruel; mountain mushrooms deep-fried in light batter; charcoal-grilled *todok* (a fibrous, hairy rootlet); mountain green *kimchi*; crunchy, stalky wild greens dressed in hot and sweet vinegar sauce; and scores of others.

POSOTBOKKUM STEWED MUSHROOMS

버섯볶음

1 oz (25 g) dried Chinese mushrooms
$\frac{1}{2}$ lb (250 g) fresh mushrooms (preferably *shitake*, if available)
$\frac{1}{4}$ lb (125 g) sirloin steak
2 tablespoons soy sauce
1 teaspoon sesame oil
2 spring onions, finely chopped
2 garlic cloves, peeled, crushed, and finely chopped
1 tablespoon toasted sesame seeds
Freshly ground black pepper

$\frac{1}{2}$ onion, peeled, cut in half lengthwise, and sliced

1 carrot, peeled and cut into matchsticks
1 courgette, sliced on the diagonal
1 red or green pepper, seeded, and cut into pieces

Vegetable oil for frying
Fried egg strips for garnish

Wash and trim the dried mushrooms carefully and soak in water for 3—4 hours or longer. Drain, rinse well, squeeze out excess water, and slice. Wash the fresh mushrooms and slice. Thinly slice the steak, and combine with soy sauce, sesame oil, spring onions, garlic, sesame seeds, and black pepper.

Heat the vegetable oil in a frying pan and stir-fry the steak until brown, about 3—5 minutes. Then add the dried mushrooms, fresh mushrooms, onion, carrot, courgette, and red or green pepper. Mix well, and cook for another 5 minutes or so, or until the vegetables are tender, but still 'al dente'. Transfer to a platter and garnish with egg strips.

AL-TCHIM STEAMED EGG

알찜

Steamed egg, flavoured with ground pork, prawn, and spring onions, is one of our old favourites, simple but satisfying. If you don't have a steamer, improvise with a covered dish placed on a rack in a larger covered pot or wok.

$\frac{1}{4}$ lb (125 g) lean ground pork
1 garlic clove, peeled, crushed, and finely chopped
1 tablespoon soy sauce
1 teaspoon sesame oil
Freshly ground black pepper
2 oz (50 g) prawns, cooked and peeled
2 spring onions, finely chopped
4 eggs
A little water

Mix the ground pork with the garlic, soy sauce, sesame oil, and black pepper. In a small pot or casserole, fry the meat mixture lightly, then add the peeled prawns and sliced spring onions. Beat the eggs with a little water and pour them over the meat and prawn mixture. Cover and place pot in a steamer and steam until the egg sets, about 20—25 minutes.

SUNDUBU-TCHIGE FRESH BEAN CURD STEW

순두부찌개

The Kamchon, located behind the American Embassy, enjoys a considerable reputation among foreign expatriates as a gathering place to meet and exchange news and stories, while downing countless bottles of Crown *maekchu*, together with bowls of a fantastically hot and delicious *sundubu-tchige*. *Sundubu* is fresh bean curd; soft, milky white curds rather like poached or lightly scrambled egg, served in sizzling stone bowls containing a pungent *kochujang* broth, fresh chillies, clams, vegetables, and egg. It is certainly the sort of food which helps promote a healthy and considerable thirst.

Fresh bean curd is not difficult to make, and is definitely worth the effort.

6 oz (175 g) yellow soy beans
Juice of 1 lemon

½ lb (250 g) pork, trimmed and cut into thin strips
2 tablespoons *kochujang*
1–3 teaspoons red pepper powder, or to taste
4 garlic cloves, peeled, crushed, and finely chopped
1 tablespoon sesame oil
1 tablespoon vegetable oil
8–12 clams in the shell, cleaned and soaked (if available)
2 courgettes, sliced on the diagonal
4–6 fresh chillies, seeded and sliced
4 spring onions, shredded on the diagonal
2 eggs, beaten, fried, and cut into thin stips

To make the *sundubu*, soak the soy beans in water overnight. Drain, and place half the soaked beans in a food processor or blender. Add a cup (about ½ pint/300 ml) of water and process or blend for 1–2 minutes or until well chopped. Strain through a fine sieve, reserving both the liquid and the pulp. Repeat with the remaining beans. Place the reserved pulp back in the food processor blender, add another cup of water and blend again for 1–2 minutes, and strain this liquid into the first liquid. The pulp can now be discarded. This thickish white liquid is soy milk.

Now bring the soy milk to a boil, reduce the heat to a simmer and cook for 15–20 minutes, stirring from time to time. Remove from the heat, and add the lemon juice. The soy milk should curdle into *sundubu* straight away. Drain off excess liquid by straining through muslin or cheesecloth, and transfer the curds to a bowl. *Sundubu* should be used immediately, or the same day that it is made.

To make the *sundubu-tchige*, mix the pork strips with the *kochujang*, red pepper powder, garlic, and sesame oil. Heat some vegetable oil in a pot or casserole, and stir-fry the meat for 5 minutes. Pour on about ¾ pint (450 ml) of water, stir to mix well, and bring to a simmer. Add the clams (if using), courgettes, fresh chillies, and spring onions (reserving a few for garnish), cook for a further 2–3 minutes, then add the *sundubu*. These soft bean curds take only a few minutes to cook. Garnish with egg strips and a few reserved spring onions. Serve at once, sizzling hot.

TUBUJORIM BEAN CURD WITH PORK AND CHILLI SAUCE

두부조림

Tubujorim is a good example of typical Korean home cooking. Not only is this bean curd dish delicious, it is also very attractive when carefully presented. Yet it is so easy and quick to prepare.

2 meaty loin pork chops on the bone (about ½ lb/250 g), trimmed of fat
2 cakes firm bean curd
2 tablespoons flour
Vegetable oil for frying

---

2 garlic cloves, peeled, crushed, and finely chopped
1 in (2.5 cm) piece of fresh ginger, peeled, crushed, and finely chopped
1½ tablespoons *kochujang*
2 tablespoons soy sauce
2 tablespoons sugar
1 tablespoon sesame oil
1 teaspoon toasted sesame seeds
Freshly ground black pepper

---

1 tablespoon vegetable oil
3 spring onions, shredded on the diagonal

Slice the pork chops into very thin slivers on the diagonal. Place the bones and trimmings in a pan, and add a little water to make some meat broth.

Slice the *tubu* cakes horizontally to divide into 2, then cut each piece again into thirds. Heat some oil in a frying pan. Dredge the *tubu* in flour on each side and fry in hot oil until brown, about 3—5 minutes a side. Drain on kitchen paper.

In a bowl, mix together the garlic, ginger, *kochujang*, soy sauce, sugar, sesame oil, sesame seeds, and pepper. Add the meat to this mixture and mix well. Heat 1 tablespoon vegetable oil in a frying pan. Add the meat mixture and cook over medium heat for about 10—15 minutes, or until cooked through. Add a little of the meat broth or water to the sauce to keep it a fairly liquid consistency. Transfer to a dish and set aside.

Layer the fried *tubu* slices in a frying pan. Spoon the meat sauce carefully over each slice. Cover and heat through over a very low flame for about 5—10 minutes or until warm, adding a little more boiling water or meat broth if necessary to keep from sticking. Transfer carefully to a serving dish and garnish with the shredded spring onions.

TUBUBUCHIM FRIED BEAN CURD

두부부침

In Korea, bean curd is such an essential part of the daily diet that it is still purchased fresh daily from door-to-door vendors who come by at least once a day, ringing noisy brass bells. It is used extensively in soups and stews, but I think that it is delicious simply lightly fried in sesame oil, and eaten with *chojang* vinegar dipping sauce. Choose firm *tubu* if possible.

2 cakes firm bean curd
2 tablespoons flour seasoned with 1 teaspoon salt
Vegetable oil and sesame oil for frying

Slice the bean curd into $\frac{1}{4}$ in (6 mm) thick slices. Dredge in seasoned flour. Heat some vegetable oil together with a little sesame oil in a frying pan to medium hot and fry the bean curd slices until golden brown on both sides, about 5 minutes each. Drain on kitchen paper and serve with *chojang* vinegar dipping sauce.

10
Sweets

Korean meals rarely finish with sweets or cakes. Indeed, the finest and most typical way to complete a meal is with fresh fruit. Alternatively, a bowl of sweet punch made from dried persimmons, Korean pears, strawberries, or rice might be offered, a most pleasant and civilized conclusion.

Korea is blessed with a profusion of fruit: luscious strawberries from Suwon and elsewhere, apples from Taegu, sticky sweet persimmons, plums, and many other sorts. Even today, on most corners of Seoul, there are fruit stands, offering these as well as such 'exotic' (and very expensive) fruits as bananas.

But, imagine Halmoni's surprise and delight with the fruits that were available and abundant when she arrived in Hawaii. The first time she saw a pineapple, she did not know what it was: but when she tasted it, she thought it was the most delicious thing she had ever eaten. There were other tropical fruits: mangoes, cigar mangoes, Indian mangoes, papayas, bananas, mountain apples and highly perfumed rose apples, loquats, avocados (always eaten with sugar), guavas, pomegranates, and persimmons.

My mother remembers that whenever Halmoni's friends came to visit, they never drank tea or coffee: rather, she would be ordered into the kitchen to slice oranges into wedges, a great mound of them that the women sucked noisily as they nattered and gossiped. Oranges are not native to Hawaii, and perhaps for that reason they were even more special a treat.

However, elaborate and delicious rice cakes and other sweets are prepared and enjoyed, particularly for special family occasions: a first birthday, the New Year, a wedding, or other great feasts.

These brightly coloured and carefully made sweets are as attractive to look at as they are to eat.

HWAJON SWEET FRIED RICE CAKES

화 전

Fried Korean rice cakes: chewy and delicious!

4 oz (125 g) glutinous rice flour
½ teaspoon salt
2 tablespoons sugar
About 6 tablespoons warm water
About 40 pine nuts
Parsley or celery leaves for decoration
Vegetable oil for frying
2 tablespoons sugar

Sift the flour, salt, and sugar into a bowl. Add enough warm water to make a stiff dough. Knead well, then form into small balls. Flatten each ball to make cookies. Decorate each with pine nuts and parsley or celery leaves pressed flat into the dough. Fry on under side in a small amount of vegetable oil until brown, about 5 minutes. Then turn and cook the decorated side briefly (about 2–3 minutes), taking care not to brown. While the cakes are still warm, sprinkle with sugar.

SONGPYON STEAMED HALF-MOON RICE CAKES

송 편

Steamed half-moon rice cakes, stuffed with mashed beans, chestnuts, or sesame seeds and honey are a popular and delicious sweet for special and festive occasions. Traditionally, half the cakes would be coloured with mugwort, a most attractive green, and they would all be steamed on beds of pine needles both to keep them separate and to impart a distinctive but delicate resiny flavour.

12 oz (350 g) glutinous rice flour
About ⅓–½ pint (200–300 ml) boiling water

---

2 oz (50 g) red beans
2 tablespoons sugar
1 teaspoon cinnamon

---

3 tablespoons prepared chestnut purée (see recipe on p. 175 or use tinned)
1 tablespoon honey

---

1 oz (25 g) toasted sesame seeds
1½ tablespoons honey
1 teaspoon salt
1 tablespoon sesame oil

Make a stiff dough with the glutinous rice flour and sufficient boiling water. Knead well, then wrap in a clean cloth to prevent the dough from drying out.

Soak the red beans in tepid water for 2 hours. Cook in boiling water until soft. Mash the beans, then pass through a coarse strainer. Add the sugar and cinnamon. Mix the chestnut purée with the honey. Mix the toasted sesame seeds with honey and salt.

Divide the dough into 3 equal parts. Break off bite-size pieces of dough, roll to flatten and fill alternately with a teaspoon of each different filling. Shape into half-moons, pinching the edges to close. When all are filled, arrange in an oiled steamer and steam for about 30 minutes or until cooked through. Remove and brush with sesame oil. Arrange in an attractive pattern on a platter and serve warm.

First Birthday

To Koreans, the first birthday is a celebration of considerable importance. On this momentous day, the baby is dressed in special multi-coloured finery and placed on a pillow in front of a low table laid out with uncooked rice, noodles, books, coins and calligraphy brushes. All the elders in the family are gathered to bring good luck and longevity to the young one; the objects are symbolic of what the future holds.

Halmoni says that Uncle Donald chose the calligraphy brush (he is a composer); Uncle John chose money (he is a doctor); Uncle Larry chose books (he is a teacher); and my mother Lori, a writer, chose rice, the symbol of good luck. Afterwards, naturally, there is a great feast, but the main foods eaten, says Halmoni, are seaweed soup and *chalttok* − sweet rice mixed with red beans, dishes symbolic of longevity.

On Guy's first birthday, we had already returned from Korea, and had rented a *gîte* in Provence. Nonetheless, we dressed him in the motley suit (*paji, chogori*, waistcoat, hat and socks) that we had purchased in Seoul, and laid out his birthday table, confidently expecting him to choose the pen or brush. To our surprise, he went straight for the pile of coins. 'Wonderful!' said his grandfather, Kim's father, when he heard of this: 'He'll be an industrialist!'

YAKSHIK SWEET SPICED RICE

약 식

Yakshik is a Korean classic, sticky glutinous rice flavoured with nuts and raisins, jujubes, sugar, soy sauce, and spices. In fact, though served as a special dessert, it is considered to be medicinal (the word *yak* means medicine).

4 cups glutinous rice
12 fresh chestnuts
20 jujubes
2 oz (50 g) pine nuts
2 tablespoons raisins
6 oz (175 g) brown sugar
3 tablespoons soy sauce
2 tablespoons sesame oil
$\frac{1}{2}$ teaspoon cinnamon

Wash the rice in several changes of water, then soak for 3—4 hours. Rinse well, drain, then place in a pot together with 5 cups of water and steam for 25—30 minutes.

Meanwhile, boil the chestnuts, peel, skin, and cut them into quarters. Pit the jujubes and cut into quarters.

Put the steamed rice into a large bowl and mix thoroughly with the chestnuts, jujubes, pine nuts, raisins, brown sugar, soy sauce, sesame oil, and cinnamon. Pack the mixture firmly in the bowl or basin, cover, and place in a steamer. Steam for a further 30 minutes, stirring from time to time. The mixture is ready to eat when the rice is very soft and sticky, and a rich dark brown colour. Serve warm, decorated with a few more pine nuts.

SAENGGANGJONGGWA CANDIED GINGER

생강정과

Candied ginger, a Korean favourite, is also much loved by the English!

4 oz (125 g) fresh ginger, peeled and very thinly sliced
4 oz (125 g) sugar
6 tablespoons water

Place the ginger in a pot and cover with water. Boil for 20−30 minutes or until tender. Drain.

In a separate pot, add the sugar and 6 tablespoons of water. Boil to form a syrup, then add the ginger. Cook slowly, until the syrup is absorbed and the ginger is well glazed. Lay out on a rack to cool, and serve as a crunchy candy.

CANDIED CHESTNUTS

밤강정

Korean *marron glacé*: a delicious favourite.

2 dozen fresh chestnuts
6 tablespoons honey
6 tablespoons water
$\frac{1}{4}$ teaspoon cinnamon

Boil the chestnuts in their shells for about 20−25 minutes or until just tender. Remove, drain, and peel off the shells and inner skin. Mix the honey and water in a pot over a low flame. Add the chestnuts and cook until all the syrup has been absorbed and the chestnuts are all well coated. Sprinkle them with a little cinnamon.

YAKKWA LITTLE HONEY CAKES

약 과

4 oz (125 g) flour
2 tablespoons sesame oil
2 tablespoons honey
2 tablespoons rice wine or dry sherry
1 teaspoon fresh ginger juice
1 teaspoon salt
1 teaspoon cinnamon
Grated rind of $\frac{1}{2}$ lemon
About 6 tablespoons water
Vegetable oil for deep frying
2 teaspoons sesame seeds

Sift the flour into a bowl. Add the sesame oil, honey, rice wine, ginger juice, salt, cinnamon, lemon rind, and sufficient water to make a smooth dough. Knead well, then roll the dough out to a thickness of $\frac{1}{4}$ in (6 mm), and cut into $1\frac{1}{2}$ in (3.5 cm) rounds with a cake cutter (in Korea, special *yakkwa* moulds are used).

Heat the oil to nearly smoking and deep-fry the cakes a few at a time until they float and have turned a light brown colour, about 3–5 minutes. Drain on kitchen paper, and sprinkle with sesame seeds.

KKAEGANGJONG SESAME CAKES

깨강정

2 oz (50 g) black sesame seeds
2 oz (50 g) white sesame seeds
8 tablespoons golden syrup
$\frac{1}{2}$ cup light brown sugar

Heat the black and white sesame seeds in separate frying pans until they just begin to toast and pop. Mix the syrup and light brown sugar together gently in a pot until dissolved. Mix half the sugar syrup with the black sesame seeds and half with the white. Allow to cool slightly, then spread each mixture on to a sheet of wax paper, and roll out. While still warm, place the black sesame sheet on top of the white one, then roll up together like a jam roly-poly. When cool, cut into slices.

Journal Notes

The Summer House

We had heard of Halmoni's childhood summer house for years and years, a dreamy dwelling in the mountains of Kyongsangbuk-do, where the family lived when they were not in Pusan. The summer house was thatched, she said, and there were three main compounds: the saranbang *(the master's quarter, where Halmoni's father — our great-grandfather — slept and entertained his friends); the* anbang *(the domain of Halmoni's mother, where she and all the girl children slept and lived — men were never allowed to enter); and a storeroom area. Little Mother (great-grandfather's second wife) slept and lived in a little room next to the* saranbang. *Halmoni remembers the groves of persimmon, gingko, chestnut and other fruit trees.*

Halmoni's summer house always seemed to us a place from another world, another era. Did it really exist? We were delighted when cousin Bong Tae offered to take us there when we met up in Pusan. Places that have long existed only in imagination are usually disappointing in reality, but not in this instance. It was just as she had described (though the thatched roof had since been replaced with corrugated iron). An oasis, high above and far away from the traffic noise and hurly-burly of Pusan, with the little village of Sochang below, it was more beautiful than any dream could have invented. Perhaps it was even more special because of the contrast it presented between an ancient and traditional way of life amid the modern, bustling, developing nation that is Korea today.

YULLAN CHESTNUT BALLS

율 란

30 chestnuts
5 tablespoons honey
1 tablespoon cinnamon
5 tablespoons pine nuts

Boil the chestnuts in their shells for 30–40 minutes, until very tender and soft. Remove, drain, and peel the shells and inner skin. Mash the peeled chestnuts into a purée and add the honey and cinnamon. Chop the pine nuts finely. Shape the chestnut mixture into small balls then roll in the chopped pine nuts.

MAEJAKKWA CAKE TWISTS

매작과

4 oz (125 g) flour
1 teaspoon salt
1½ tablespoons sugar
3 tablespoons rice wine or dry sherry
About 6 tablespoons water
Vegetable oil for deep frying
8 tablespoons honey mixed with 4 tablespoons water
2 tablespoons pine nuts, chopped

Sift the flour, salt, and sugar into a bowl. Add the rice wine and sufficient water to make a smooth dough. Knead well, then roll out into thin sheets and cut into pieces 2 in (5 cm) long by ¼ in (6 mm) wide. Slit each piece down the centre leaving both ends intact and pull one end of each piece through the slit to make a twist. Heat the oil to nearly smoking and deep-fry the cakes until crisp. Gently warm the honey and dip in each cake, then sprinkle with pine nuts.

A Few Wedding Customs

Halmoni remembers that whenever one of her sisters left to get married, all the women would sit together in the *anbang* and cry all night. These were some of the wedding customs that used to take place:

● The bride was not allowed to smile on her wedding day. If she did, then she was sure to have a daughter.

● The groom was not allowed to smile either and had to withstand excessive teasing about how good his wife would be in bed.

● The groom always rode a horse into the courtyard the day of the wedding. Unmarried girls were not allowed to look at him, but they used to poke holes in the paper screens to peek.

● The day after the wedding, the bride's family was allowed to throw the groom on his stomach, bind his legs together, and beat the soles of his bare feet, demanding 'How much money are you going to pay?'

PAESUK PEAR PUNCH

배 숙

The Korean or Asian pear is quite different from our pears: brown, thick-skinned, very crisp, juicy, and sweet. It is now quite widely available from speciality greengrocers.

1 in (2.5 cm) piece of fresh ginger, peeled, and thinly sliced
2 pints (1 litre) water
1 Korean pear
5 tablespoons sugar
Pine nuts to garnish

Place the sliced ginger in a pot and cover with the water. Bring to the boil and simmer for 30 minutes. Remove and discard the ginger. Peel and core the Korean pear and cut it into segments. Add to the saucepan together with the sugar and simmer lightly for another 20–30 minutes. Remove from the heat, transfer to a jug, and chill well in the refrigerator. Serve as a drink in individual glass bowls, with a few slices of pear in each bowl, decorated with 4 or 5 pine nuts floating on the surface.

SUJONGGWA PERSIMMON PUNCH

수 정과

Halmoni remembers the groves of persimmon trees that covered the slopes around the summer house in Sochang. In autumn the fruit was harvested and enjoyed fresh, as well as dried to be used later. This persimmon punch is made from slices of dried persimmons.

1 in (2.5 cm) piece of fresh ginger, peeled and thinly sliced
2 pints (1 litre) water
5 tablespoons sugar
10 dried persimmons
½ teaspoon cinnamon
1 tablespoon pine nuts

Add the sliced ginger to a large pot and pour over the water. Bring to the boil and simmer for about 30 minutes. Remove the ginger and discard. Add the sugar and continue to cook until dissolved. Meanwhile, wash the dried persimmons and trim away the woody stems. Add to the ginger and sugar water and cook for a further 30 minutes. Remove from the heat, cover, and set aside in a cool place overnight. Serve in bowls, one persimmon in each, with juice spooned over. Garnish each bowl with a little cinnamon and pine nuts.

TTALGIHWACHAE STRAWBERRY PUNCH

딸기화채

In early summer, the strawberries from places such as Suwon are particularly delicious, and restaurants all over the country devise special 'strawberry menus'. When just ripe, however, we think they are best simply eaten on their own. But when less than perfect, then they are best utilized to make this simple strawberry punch.

12–15 large strawberries
6 tablespoons sugar, or to taste
2 pints (1 litre) water
1 tablespoon pine nuts

Wash and hull the strawberries and cut into thin slices. Boil the sugar and water together to form a syrup, then leave to cool. Place the sliced strawberries in a large bowl and pour over the syrup. Cover and place in a refrigerator and leave to soak and soften for several hours. To serve, ladle into individual glass bowls and garnish with pine nuts.

Journal Notes

Hang a Lantern for Buddha

Haeinsa, Korea's most famous Buddhist temple, is marvellously atmospheric and peaceful, especially today as the mist drifted down from the Kaya mountain peaks, and the wavy-patterned slate-grey roofs of the monastic buildings stood out against an even darker sky. This monochromatic image was sharply relieved by the scores of brightly coloured paper lanterns hanging throughout the temple complex in readiness for Buddha's birthday, a moveable feast which occurs annually on the eighth day of the fourth lunar month, some time between late April and mid May.

We wandered in awe and reverence through this holy place, the repository for the Tripitaka, a magnificent collection of over eighty thousand wood blocks hand-carved with Buddhist scripture. Monks glided by, their grey robes swishing lightly before they disappeared behind paper screen doors.

At the main temple, the Taejokkwangjon, some monks were sitting inside by the entrance. As we admired the vast and colourful interior, they beckoned us over, wanting to talk and to look at Guy. One in particular, a kind-faced, large and gentle man, held Guy up to his face, and the others laughed heartily — we assumed because our five-month-old baby was as bald as the monk's own shaved and shiny pate.

Our new friend then suggested that I hang a lantern in the temple for Guy: indeed I was most honoured. First, I wrote out Guy's name on a paper ribbon, then I took off my shoes and entered the temple with the monk. Placing my palms together, I bowed deeply in front of the gilt statue of the Bodhisattva as instructed, then attached Guy's ribbon to a maroon lantern near the altar.

While inside that temple, I was overwhelmed by a sense of hope and peace. That feeling was all the more intense in the knowledge that some weeks later, back home in England, I would remember this lantern, hanging among a thousand others far away in central Korea, to be lit on Buddha's birthday this year of 1988, giving blessing for long life and happiness to our son.

SHIKYE SWEET RICE DRINK

식 혜

Shikye is a classic: a favourite Korean sweet rice drink offered after the meal. In the past, sugar was not widely available as a sweetener so malt was used instead.

6 oz (175 g) malt
4 pints (2 litres) lukewarm water
12 oz (350 g) glutinous rice
Sugar to taste
Pine nuts

Mix the malt with the lukewarm water and leave to stand over-night, stirring occasionally. Strain through muslin or a very fine sieve and reserve the malt water.

Wash the glutinous rice in several changes of water. Soak for 3–4 hours. Place in a rice cooker (or a pot) and add 1 pint (600 ml) cold water. Bring to the boil, cover, and steam for 25 minutes. When cooked, pour on sufficient strained malt water to come nearly to the top of the pot. Stir well, then cover tightly. Keep the rice cooker on warm (or the pot over a very low fire), and leave for 2 hours or so, until the rice grains begin to float on the surface. When this happens, transfer to a container and allow to cool. Add sugar to taste (it should already be quite sweet from the malt water). Serve in individual bowls with a few grains of rice and pine nuts floating on the surface.

11
Drink

Koreans, it has to be said, are great tipplers. Indeed drinking has been an institutionalized way of life and the traditional pursuit of both nobleman and commoner for centuries. Finely wrought gold- and silver-decorated wine cups; stoneware, horn-shaped double wine cups; wine cups with covers and pedestal stands: the profusion of such artefacts dating from the Three Kingdoms period (57 BC—AD 668) and earlier demonstrates the long-established importance of drinking, certainly for the privileged and royal classes. The first public folk tavern, however, was reputedly built in Kaesong in 1102; presumably this was a wayside inn that brewed and produced its own rice wine and *makkolli* and served simple foods and drinking snacks. Since that date, Koreans have never looked back: today there are *sul-jib* — bars or drinking houses — on virtually every street corner in the country.

Undoubtedly there is a certain formality to proceedings when Koreans gather to drink, a throw-back to the Yi dynasty when neo-Confucian codes dictated all social interaction, relationships, and behaviour. Protocol demands, for example, that you never drink alone. Moreover, it is the height of bad form ever to pour a drink for yourself. Rather, you are offered your drinking partner's cup (always with both hands) which he fills for you; you are expected to down the cup, return it, and then pour him a drink in turn (again using both hands). Though undoubtedly such rituals were originally based on precepts of mutual hospitality, they now can lead, inevitably, to hearty one-upmanship and the forcing of drinks on one another to the point of virtual leglessness.

Drinking has been the preserve of the Korean male for centuries. Indeed, men in their private *sarangbangs* would while away the hours and days sipping rice wine from cups the colour of a kingfisher's crest or the sky after rain. They might have been accompanied or entertained, perhaps, by a favourite *kisaeng*. But this exception apart, women traditionally were not expected to drink or to be seen drinking.

Even today, drinking remains mainly the preserve of the Korean male, though women are allowed to enter bars and drink in public. Uncle Donald lived in Seoul in the early seventies, the period when martial law had been declared, ostensibly for reasons of national security. They were, he recalls with a rueful smile, good times, spent with his drinking cronies inevitably whiling the nights away until well past the midnight curfew when all citizens were ordered to clear the streets. There were many comic — but potentially tragic — moments as they stumbled back to their houses, moving from shadow to shadow for fear of being apprehended. If caught, after all, they could have been shot on sight.

Why did they take such risks, just for another few cups of throat-burning liquor? There is a single phrase in Korean — *kong cho* — which roughly translates 'man who is afraid of wife'. Donald and his drinking mates, and all the other men huddled in *soju* tents and *makkolli-jib* of Seoul and elsewhere, are desperately trying to prove to each other that they are not. Don't you believe it. To a man, they are terrified. If you have ever seen an enraged Korean wife (or mother or grandmother) in action, you will know that they have every reason to be. It is an awesome sight.

Makkolli traditionally has been the mainstay of the working man. A cloudy, rough, frothing, milky-white beverage brewed from rice, it is something of an acquired taste. Of course, there is *makkolli*, and *makkolli*, say *aficionados*, the best examples of which are available only in the country outside the capital. Nonetheless, *makkolli* — like Mexican *pulque*, which it somewhat resembles — is a classic and centuries-old drink of the land, still highly popular.

More common still is *soju*, a clear distilled liquor produced primarily from grains other than rice, mainly rye and sweet potatoes. Somewhat sweet in flavour and seemingly innocuous to the first-time drinker, *soju* has an alcoholic content of little more than 20—25 per cent, but as it is sold in beer-size, blue-tinted bottles costing less than a pound or so each, it is indeed not difficult to get carried away in an evening, to your considerable regret the next morning. My sister Michele thought *soju* tasted just like surgical spirit (some might say she is being over-complimentary); but I actually grew quite fond of the stuff — in small doses.

Korean beer — *maekju* — is widely available. There are two principal brands, OB and Crown, both of which are light, lager

---

Posokchong: The Abalone Stone Drinking Bower

On the outskirts of Kyongju, on the gentle slopes of Nam-san some distance from the famous burial mounds, the National Museum and the other venues which coachloads of tourists and school-children rush madly to and from each day, there is a quiet, isolated oasis where, under the shade of an age-old gingko tree, lies an unusual shell-shaped stone channel. This is Posokchong, the abalone stone drinking bower. The stone channel is all that is left of a former royal pleasure pavilion where Silla kings retired in summer to drink wine, dally with their favourite *kisaeng*, or compose poetry.

The king, princes, and other members of the aristocratic ruling class would sit around this shaded drinking bower while water from a nearby stream was diverted into the stone channel. The sounds of music and song mingled with the gentle trickle of water. As the men lay or rested by the stone channel, they floated cups on the moving waters and when they passed by, each person in turn had to compose a spontaneous poem before his cup reached a certain bend. Those who failed had the far from unpleasant forfeit of having to down their cup.

The last Silla king, Kyongae, was here, amusing himself in this fashion, careless of concerns or affairs of state, when his capital was attacked and sacked. He was murdered on this very spot in the midst of his reveries. So ended a thousand years of Silla rule. This modest, stone drinking bower may well suggest the decadent and indolent lives that the ruling classes led during the later and declining years of Silla; I prefer to view it as a monument to a way of thinking — indeed to an entire civilization — that placed greater emphases on poetry, aesthetics and drinking wine, than on the martial arts.

---

types. Korean beer — indeed most beers — I think, goes particularly well with Korean food.

Tong dong ju is a popular country rice wine, usually not all that refined in colour, clarity, or flavour, but sometimes outstanding. *Nong ju* is the name for a similar 'farmer's wine' available mainly in the south. *Chung chong ju*, on the other hand, is a sort of Korean sake often served warm in china carafes. *Pob ju*, particularly that brewed in Kyongju, is the finest rice wine available, a very high quality alcoholic drink that is clear, refined and delicious. *Pob ju* sold in restaurants, however, is usually very expensive.

Korean grape wines are also now being produced in small quantities. Though nowhere as fine as their New World or

European counterparts, they can be quite satisfactory nonetheless. We particularly enjoyed Majuang, a dry white Riesling which, though neither delicate nor subtle, had enough body and robust flavour to stand up well to highly seasoned Korean foods.

Finally, there are a number of 'tonic' wines that are taken, ostensibly for reasons of health or flagging powers. *Insam ju* — ginseng wine — is the most common, and indeed a tot of this earthy, distinctive liquor really is a most potent pick-me-up.

One other particularly Korean institution must be mentioned, the *tabang*, or coffee house. Everybody in Korea — students, housewives, business men, lovers — have their favourite *tabang*. Like the coffee houses of old Vienna, they are far more than mere places to consume a cup of coffee (often it is only instant) or tea. In an overcrowded and always crowded nation, they are places where you stake out your pitch, settle down — for a quarter of an hour or for several hours — seeing and being seen, meeting friends, carrying on a business conversation, plotting a political coup, or pulsating in anticipation of an amorous rendezvous. Each *tabang* caters for its own clientele (many play music — almost always very loudly), but the atmosphere is usually congenial and unhurried.

The Kisaeng

Kisaengs, especially during the Yi dynasty, were cultured concubines who existed for the pleasure of the male *yangban* aristocrats and royal courtiers. Generally these legendary, beautiful women came from the very lowest classes, but they were by no means mere instruments of sensual pleasure. *Kisaengs* underwent rigorous education and training and were expected to be versed in the skills of poetry, dance, song, calligraphy and horse riding. Naturally, they also learned the art of satisfying the demands and physical pleasures of those men for whom they worked.

Today, only a few *kisaeng* houses remain, and the *kisaeng*, by all accounts, no longer possess the same degree of culture and skills as their famous predecessors. Yet, what I find most fascinating about the *kisaeng* of old is that in a rigid, male-dominated neo-Confucian society, these women were able to attain the highest levels of culture and education and lead lives apparently relatively free from the rigid constraints imposed upon other women of their era. In a sense, though social outcasts, they were at the same time considered the equals of — perhaps in some instances even superior to — the men they served.

Uncle Donald had urged us to visit his old hangout, The Cosy Corner Tabang in Myong-dong. We were to send his regards to 'Kim Madame', owner and famous fortune-teller. Donald had not been there for over twenty years, but was sure that she would remember him. My cousin in Seoul, Bong Tae, brightened up at this request. He knew her well himself, and would make a personal reservation for 'Kim Madame' to meet us and read our fortunes (apparently she does not do this for all and sundry — only for friends and regular customers). But unfortunately, this was not to be. The Cosy Corner was closed while we were in Seoul; like the rest of the city, it too was being remodelled in preparation for the Olympics.

PORICHA ROASTED BARLEY TEA

보 리 차

Poricha is the ubiquitous beverage offered in Korean homes, inns, and restaurants alike. Though it has a distinctive flavour that perhaps is not immediately appealing, the taste does grow on you for it is a most thirst quenching drink, served either hot, luke-warm, or cold with sugar or honey. Roasted barley is available from Korean groceries.

4 tablespoons roasted barley
3 pints (1½ litres) water

Soak the barley in the water for 30 minutes, then bring to the boil and simmer for about an hour or longer. Pour through a sieve into a teapot. Drink hot, warm, or — especially in summer — chilled with a dollop of honey in it.

SUNGNYUNG RICE TEA

숭 늉

Rice tea, made by simply boiling water with the dregs of the burnt rice left-over in the pot, may hardly sound like a promising concoction. Yet this humble beverage, pale, opaque, with little colour or flavour is an authentic and genuine flavour of Korea, much loved by all.

Dregs of burnt rice left-over in the pot after cooking
About 2 pints (1 litre) water

Add the water to the burnt rice in the rice pot, and bring to a boil. Leave to simmer for about 15—20 minutes, then pour into mugs at the end of a meal.

Journal Notes

City Centre Tear Gas

Returned to Seoul yesterday, and looked out from the twelfth floor window of our hotel room this morning to witness a bizarre scene. Traffic along busy Taepyong-no had been brought to a complete standstill as thousands marched along the street, waving, chanting, carrying banners and flags. A few days earlier, a young student had stabbed himself then jumped off Myong-dong Cathedral to his death, leaving behind a list of demands, including immediate reunification with the North. This demonstration was his funeral procession, as well as a public show of support for those demands.

We watched for a while, then made our way to Myong-dong, Seoul's Times Square. As we passed through a pedestrian subway we suddenly felt the sharp sting of tear gas. People rushed down the stairs, eyes red and streaming, clutching handkerchiefs over their faces. We followed the crowds, and escaped into the basement entrance of the Lotte Department Store.

From an upstairs window, we watched in disbelief as scenes we had witnessed only on television were re-enacted before our eyes. The Army, with their riot helmets, padded body armour, shields and big sticks, moved in. The tear-gas grenades exploded, and students hurled rocks and make-shift incendiary devices.

The well-dressed shoppers in the Lotte had little sympathy for the rioters and people apologized to us, apparently embarrassed that we should have been caught up in this unsightly incident. I could not help but be reminded of Halmoni, some seventy years earlier, caught up in the emotion of a similar demonstration against the Japanese, that morning in March 1919.

INSAMCHA GINSENG TEA

생강차

Insam — ginseng — of course is a general panacea, taken widely by all and for any manner of ailments. Though ginseng is available in tea bags, the best ginseng tea is made either from freshly boiled roots, or else by steeping slices of red ginseng, the most potent manifestation of this very special 'man root'. Ginseng has a distinctive flavour that is actually quite delicious and addictive.

4–6 slices red ginseng
6 jujubes
1 in (2.5 cm) piece of fresh ginger, sliced
3 pints (1½ litres) water

Place the sliced red ginseng, jujubes, and ginger in a pot, add the water and bring to the boil. Reduce to a simmer, cover, and cook for 1 hour or longer. Serve in cups with a slice of ginseng, jujube, and piece of ginger in each.

SAENGGANGCHA GINGER TEA

인삼차

3 oz (90 g) fresh ginger, peeled, and very thinly sliced
Twist of fresh orange peel
2 jujubes
3 pints (1½ litres) water
4 tablespoons honey
½ teaspoon cinnamon
1 tablespoon pine nuts

Boil the ginger in the water with the orange peel and jujubes for about 30 minutes. Remove the ginger and orange peel and add the honey and cinnamon. Serve in cups garnished with a shake of cinnamon and a few floating pine nuts.

Journal Notes

Chongno 5-ga

I was most disappointed when we finally had a chance to explore Chongno 5-ga, the street opposite Tongdaemun Sijang famous for its hanyak *— traditional medicine shops. It seems that in this year of the Olympics, the authorities have deemed that this is not a feature of modern Korea that they want the world to see. Thus, though one can smell the rich and pungent aroma of herb, root, and animal essences being boiled and extracted, the shops themselves look very ordinary indeed from the outside, the more vivid manifestations having been removed from public gaze: live snakes and reptiles, rhinoceros horn, or dried sea turtle penis (not that I would have recognized the latter — dried or otherwise). I had steeled myself to sampling a yellow python or albino snake broth — I have, after all, been feeling somewhat lethargic lately — but, unfortunately, the opportunity did not present itself. Perhaps on my next visit?*

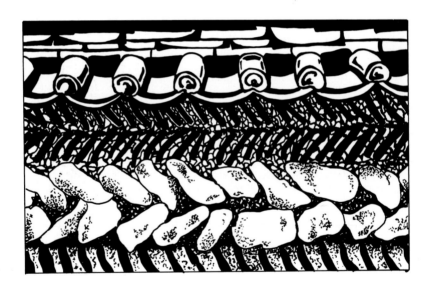

Appendix

Appendix: Selected Korean Groceries and Restaurants in Britain

Please note that many Korean ingredients may be purchased at Chinese or other oriental grocers.

Grocers

Han Kook Supermarket
20 Coombe Road
Kingston Upon Thames
Surrey KT2 7AG
tel: 081−549 6387

Seoul Foodmarket
113 Burlington Road
New Malden
Surrey KT3 4LR
tel: 081−942 8471

Han Yung Grocer
202−204 Merton High Street
South Wimbledon
London SW19
tel: 081−542 8343

Restaurants

Shilla Restaurant
58−59 Great Marlborough St
London W1V 1DD
tel: 071−434 1650

Koryo Restaurant
56 St Giles High Street
London WC2H 8NN
tel: 071−836 7235

Mimi Korean Restaurant
116 Newgate Street
London EC1A 7AE
tel: 071−606 2320

Arirang Korean Restaurant
31−32 Poland Street
London W1V 3DB
tel: 071−437 6633

Restaurant Kaya
22−25 Dean Street
London W1 5AL
tel: 071−734 2720

Koreana Restaurant
40a King Street West
Manchester M3 2WY
tel: 061−832 4330

Youna Korean Restaurant
54 Portland Street
Manchester N1 4QU
tel: 061−236 0783

Arirang House
of Knightsbridge
Arirang House
3 Park Close
Knightsbridge
London SW1X 7PQ
tel: 071−581 1820, 071−584 7794

Cho Won Korean Restaurant
27 Romilly Street
London W1V 5TQ
tel: 071−437 2262, 071−734 2227

Han Il Kwan
48 Holbom Viaduct
London EC1
tel: 071−583 5266

Allpace Ltd Seoul Restaurant
89A Aldgate High Street
London EC3 1LH
tel: 071−480 5770

Youme House
510A Homsey Road,
London N19
tel: 071−272 6208, 071−485 7899

Kangnam Korean Restaurant
178 Upper Richmond Road
West East Sheen
London SW14
tel: 081−876 9063

Nightneat Limited T/A Young Bin K
3 St Alphage Highwalk
Barbican
London EC2Y 5EL
tel: 071−638 9151, 071−628 0492

Select Bibliography

Adams, Edward B., *Korea's Kyongju*. Seoul International Publishing House, 1986.

Crane, Paul S., *Korean Patterns*. Royal Asiatic Society (Korea Branch), 1978.

Goepper, Roger, Introduction to *Treasures from Korea*, edited by Roderick Whitfield. British Museum Publications Ltd., 1984.

Han Chung Hea, *Korean Cooking*, trans. Joan Riemer. Chung Woo Publishing Co., 1983.

Hastings, Max, *The Korean War*. Michael Joseph Ltd., 1987.

Hyun, Judy, *The Korean Cookbook*. Hollym International Corp., 1979.

Kang Hong-bin, *Seoul City Guide*, Ahn Graphics, 1987.

Kim, Warren Y., *Koreans in America*. Po Chin Chai Printing Co. Ltd., 1971.

Lee Ki-baik, *A New History of Korea*, trans. Edward W. Wagner. Harvard University Press, 1984.

Lee O-Young, *In This Earth & in That Wind: This is Korea*, trans. David I. Steinberg. Royal Asiatic Society (Korea Branch), 1983.

Lueras, Leonard, and Chung, Nedra (eds.), *Korea Insight Guide*. Apa Publications, 1983.

Noh Chin-hwa, *Practical Korean Cooking*. Hollym International Corp., 1985.

Suh Hwan, *All Purpose Guide to Korean Food*. Seoul International Publishing House, 1987.

Winchester, Simon, *Korea: A Walk Through the Land of Miracles*. Grafton Books, 1988.

Index